Handbook of The Cleveland Museum of Art

Handbook of The Cleveland Museum of Art

Cleveland, Ohio/1991

Photographers: Howard T. Agriesti, Nicholas Hlobeczy, and Gary Kirchenbauer
Designers: Laurence Channing and Charles Szabla
Editors: Rachel G. Feingold and Jo Zuppan
Production Manager: Emily S. Rosen
Printers: Stinehour Press, Lunenburg, Vermont
Copyright 1991 by The Cleveland Museum of Art, Cleveland, Ohio

Library of Congress Cataloging in Publication Data
Cleveland Museum of Art
  Handbook of The Cleveland Museum of Art.
    p. cm.
  Includes index.
  ISBN 0-940717-00-x: $15.00 (est.)
  1.Art—Ohio—Cleveland—Catalogs. 2.Cleveland Museum of Art-
-Catalogs. I.Title
N552.A6 1991
708.171'32—dc20   91-11314
                CIP

The notation (detail) means that only a portion of a work of art is reproduced; in the case of Asian handscrolls this may mean only that the calligraphy accompanying an illustration has been omitted.

Where an asterisk (*) appears at the end of a credit line, this indicates that the credit line has been shortened. A list with full credit lines appears on page 161.

Cover: *The Cleveland Museum of Art,* May, 1988. Gelatin silver print. Cervin Robinson, American, b. 1928. Funded by a grant from The Cleveland Foundation and the East Ohio Gas Company. 89.498 © 1989 Cervin Robinson.

act. = active
attr. = attributed
b. = born
c. = century, centuries
ca. = circa
d. = died
D. = diameter
H. = height
L. = length
Max. = maximum
r. = reigned
W. = width

1st = first
2d = second
3d = third
4th = fourth, etc.

Contents

The Cleveland Museum of Art epitomizes the commitment repeatedly evident among the city's generous donors. It all started, as the 19th century drew to a close, when three men—Hinman B. Hurlbut, Horace Kelley, and John Huntington—each wrote wills designating the greater part of their fortunes for establishing an art museum. After more than twenty years of frustrating negotiations, ways were found to enable the three trusts to join forces without compromising their separate, legal identities, and The Cleveland Museum of Art was incorporated on July 2, 1913. Three years later, on June 6, the Museum, located near Western Reserve University upon land given by J. H. Wade, opened its doors.

At the time of incorporation the Museum possessed only 119 paintings, for the most part recent American works, collected by Mr. Hurlbut. Even before construction began, however, the Huntington Trustees made monies available for the purchase of objects in Egypt. Tentatively, the Museum's earliest supporters presented the first of the many objects needed to fill the grand galleries of the handsome Beaux-Arts building designed by Hubbell and Benes, although there was as yet little method in the collecting. The splendid loan exhibition of paintings that marked the Museum's opening could leave no doubt as to the Board's ambitious goals, and there were important gifts. Believing it appropriate in a steelmaking center, Mr. and Mrs. John L. Severance eagerly sought and acquired a large armor collection for the Museum. His sister, Elisabeth Severance Allen, presented in memory of her husband Dudley P. Allen, a suite of 17th-century tapestries, which still contributes to the imposing impact of the Armor Court. But perhaps most important, Mrs. Liberty Holden gave the Museum her collection of "early sacred paintings," many of which her husband had purchased in 1884 from the noted collector James Jackson Jarves. Then, within

weeks of the opening, the Wades gave a fine group of pictures, including examples by such contemporary masters as Monet and Degas; and shortly thereafter Mr. Wade established the Museum's initial acquisition fund.

Frederic Allen Whiting became the Museum's first Director in 1913 and served until 1930. His enthusiastic commitment to the arts and crafts of the day led to his establishing in 1919 an annual exhibition of contemporary work, the so-called *May Show*. Ever since then, with one exception, this popular exhibition has presented works created by Cleveland-area artists each year.

It is not surprising, therefore, that with the arrival in 1919 of the first Curator of Decorative Arts, William Milliken, the Cleveland Museum concentrated more upon obtaining objects than paintings. Finding a significant supporter in the Museum's second President, J. H. Wade, Mr. Milliken, who had previously worked at the Metropolitan Museum of Art in New York with J. P. Morgan's great medieval holdings, launched the acquisition of a spectacular series of medieval works. Its culmination was the purchase in 1930 and 1931 of eight pieces from Germany's famous Guelph Treasure, an extraordinary gathering of finely wrought works of art dating from the Middle Ages. Succeeding Whiting as Director in 1930, Milliken remained in charge until March 31, 1958.

With the Depression Cleveland's spiraling prosperity suffered a severe set-back, and the Museum had to retrench. Even so, it confirmed its future collecting policy by acquiring a succession of objects that, while relatively few in number, possessed great aesthetic distinction. Possibly influenced by its early commitment to education, the Museum had from the first collected works from all periods and all parts of the world. It eschewed the specialization favored by so many of its peer institutions. Local collectors, most

notably John L. Severance, who had become the Museum's third President in 1926, and his sister, by then Elisabeth Severance Prentiss, made it clear that their treasures were acquired with the needs of the Museum in mind, so the Director and Curators could concentrate upon collecting in other areas. There were as well vital support groups. The members of The Print Club of Cleveland, founded in 1919, added significantly to the collection during these slim years, while the creation of The Textile Arts Club (now called The Textile Art Alliance) in 1934 responded to the Museum's notable interest in the history of textiles (rather than costumes).

With the outbreak of World War II and Cleveland's economic recovery, the Museum's fortunes radically improved. The Severance and the Prentiss collections arrived—indeed, the individual objects looked even more distinguished when seen in the Museum galleries rather than in opulent domestic settings. They were accompanied as well by most welcome endowments, one for acquisitions and one for operations, which somewhat eased the loss of such staunch friends. Also, the Museum began to pursue paintings more aggressively because of a handsome endowment fund established for that purpose by Mrs. William H. Marlatt. As encouraging as each of these generous acts was, however, more pivotal in terms of the Museum's future was the aggressive involvement of a Cleveland bachelor who spent much of his time in New York City: Leonard C. Hanna, Jr. Just before the war he had given the Museum a group of Renaissance decorative arts objects collected by his mother, Coralie Walker Hanna; and in 1941 he established the Hanna Fund to underwrite the acquisition of major paintings by the Museum. During the 1950s along with the trustees of the original Huntington Trust and various other donors (most notably the Wades' daughter, Mrs. Edward B. Greene, and a former Clevelander,

Grace Rainey Rogers), Mr. Hanna contributed handsomely toward building a new wing. Designed by J. Byers Hays and Paul C. Ruth, it more than doubled the size of the original building. As the wing opened in March 1958, it was publicly announced that the recently deceased Mr. Hanna had bequeathed the largest sum ever given to a museum at that time, some $34,000,000. The income from the bequest was to be divided equally between acquisitions and operations.

With Sherman E. Lee as Director, the following twenty-five years were halcyon ones. For much of that time the Museum had the largest acquisition funds of any museum. With such an astute Director—as this *Handbook* amply proves—Cleveland took the fullest advantage of opportunities as they emerged throughout the world. While an earlier interest in Asian art was developed with much greater method, every area acquired significant objects during these years.

The Museum's long-standing commitment to education as well as to a developing program of special exhibitions resulted in a third major addition to the building in 1970. Marcel Breuer and Hamilton Smith designed the wing, with a flamboyant striped granite façade, wrapping around the 1958 addition. It answered the need for larger and better special exhibition galleries, classrooms, and lecture halls. It also housed Gartner Auditorium, named for Ernest L. and Louise M. Gartner, who made a substantial bequest to the Department of Musical Arts, which itself was founded in 1920 as a memorial to P. J. McMyler and is one of the first such departments in any of the world's museums.

Although the number of donors to the Museum has been small, they continue to be crucial. The tradition of collecting a variety of works of art to enhance a domestic environment was evident in one other vital gift, the collection created by Severance and Greta Millikin, which was likewise accompanied by a major acquisition fund. The more recent American trend of concentrating upon one area and pursuing it with intense energy is evident in the fine gatherings given by such people as Noah Butkin, Kelvin Smith, and the significant promised gift of the Wades' granddaughter Mrs. A. Dean Perry.

The Museum's fourth addition, designed by Dalton, van Dijk, Johnson & Partners, responded to the two greatest space needs: more galleries for 19th- and 20th-century art and a greatly expanded library. The wing's construction and installation spanned Sherman E. Lee's retirement, in 1983, and the arrival of the fourth Director, Evan H. Turner.

The holdings of The Cleveland Museum of Art are relatively few in number: some 30,000 objects. Intentionally, no study collection has been developed. Instead, all efforts have been concentrated upon building up a collection—for the most part always on view—that suggests the broad range of the history human creativity in the visual arts. It is furthermore a remarkably balanced collection, the representation of Asian art being as considered as that of Western art. This unusual character largely results from two factors peculiar to this Museum. Unlike most American museums, only a few private collections have been absorbed into its galleries; thus, the successive waves of particular enthusiasms associated with such personal holdings are hardly evident in Cleveland's Museum. It has, on the other hand, been the loser in some ways; but, without question, that so many generous Cleveland donors have given funds rather than objects has enabled the professional staff, at all times admirably supported by an interested Board of Trustees, to create the balanced collection we know today. The other significant factor pertinent to the collection is the fact that two men, William M. Milliken and Sherman E. Lee, having comparably distinguished tastes albeit perceptibly different in character, carried much of the responsibility for shaping it over sixty-four of the Museum's seventy-five years.

This seventh *Handbook* of that collection is being published to coincide with the celebrations of the Museum's seventy-fifth anniversary. Comparing it with the first *Handbook*, published in 1925, vividly brings home the collection's extraordinary growth during those intervening sixty-six years, while noting which objects have been included and then eliminated in successive editions provides a fascinating overview of its development. The earlier editions considered the collection in a more traditional fashion, grouping objects according to curatorial division, that is, ancient art, decorative arts (including African and Pre-Columbian), paintings, drawings and prints, and the arts of Asia. The most recent edition—which appeared in 1978—reflected the point-of-view evident in the then newly installed galleries. Grouping together the various kinds of objects created at roughly the same time and place, the achievements of the West were illustrated as a unit, then those of the East, with Africa, Oceania, and the work of native Americans placed at the end. However, this newest edition of the *Handbook* goes a step further, challengingly so we hope. And its new format is only possible because of the particular character of Cleveland's collection.

Given the breadth and the balance of the Museum's holdings, we have taken advantage of this opportunity to consider the objects in a way that could never be realized in the galleries. Starting with one of the earliest works, an Egyptian Predynastic *Fish-Shaped Palette* of about 3500 BC (CMA 89.32), and working steadily towards Anselm Kiefer's *Lot's Wife* of 1989 (CMA 90.8), a route has been charted through the history of art that juxtaposes all objects, regardless of origin, created at the same time. The result is fascinating. Such a cross-cultural approach discloses daring juxtapositions. At times, for example, one finds remarkably similar points-of-view appearing in widely separated parts of the world; it would, of course, be dangerous to presume direct influences in such cases, but these and other comparisons repeatedly trigger provocative considerations. As a result, this *Handbook* is, we trust, much more than just an *aide-mémoire.*

To be more specific, it provides a worldwide view of art at almost any point in time—as represented by the Cleveland collection—if the illustrations on facing pages are viewed from left to right. When appropriate, the first column on the left deals with the Americas

and then, working towards the right, successive columns sweep across the globe, first to Europe and Africa, then to the Near East, Asia, and finally Japan. Simultaneously, the Museum's holdings of material from any one country or culture can be seen in the appropriately marked vertical column on successive pages, scanning from top to bottom. The approximate dates or spans of time covered are indicated in the outer margin of the right-hand page. Broadly speaking, left-hand pages present Western art and right-hand pages Asian; inevitably, however, not only does the relative productivity of any one area vary from one period to another, but the Museum's holdings may also not be consistently extensive. Indeed, such an overview suggests provocative routes for future acquisitions!

Evan H. Turner, *Director*

Chronological Tables

These lists give the approximate dates for some of the dynasties and periods within which works of art included in this Handbook are dated.

Ancient Egypt

Predynastic to 2920 BC

Early Dynastic period (Dynasties I-III) 2920-2575 BC

Old Kingdom (Dynasties IV-VIII) 2575-2134 BC

First Intermediate period (Dynasties IX-XI) 2134-2040 BC

Middle Kingdom (Dynasties XI-XIV) 2040-1640 BC

Second Intermediate period (Dynasties XV-XVII) 1640-1550 BC

New Kingdom (Dynasties XVIII-XX) 1550-1070 BC

Third Intermediate period (Dynasties XXI-XXIV) 1070-712 BC

Late period (Dynasties XXV-XXX) 712-332 BC

Greco-Roman period 332 BC-AD 395

Cambodian Art

Pre-Angkor period AD 600-877

Angkorean period 877-1437

Indian Art

Indus Valley Civilization ca. 2500-ca. 1500 BC

Saisunaga-Nanda period 642-322 BC

Maurya period 322-185 BC

Sunga period 185-72 BC

Andhra period 70 BC-3d c. AD

Kushan period (including Gandhara) AD 50-320

Gupta period (including Harsha) 320-647

Pallava period (south) 600-750

Western Chalukya period 500-753

Rashtrakuta period 753-900

Pala and Sena periods 730-1197

Medieval Kingdoms of Rajputana and Deccan 900-1190

Chola period (south) mid 9th c.-1310

Sultanate of Delhi 1200-14th c.

Vijayanagar period (south) 1336-1646

Madura period (south) 1546-1900

Mughal dynasty 1626-1756

Rajput style 1500-1900

Chinese Art

Shang dynasty 15th c.-1027 BC

Western Zhou dynasty 1027-771 BC

Eastern Zhou dynasty 771-256 BC

    Spring and Autumn period 722-481 BC

    Warring States period 481-221 BC

Qin dynasty 221-206 BC

Western Han dynasty 206 BC-AD 9

Eastern Han dynasty AD 25-220

Three Kingdoms period 220-265

Western Qin dynasty 265-316

Six Dynasties period 220-589

    Northern Liang dynasty 397-439

    Northern Wei dynasty 386-535

    Eastern Wei dynasty 534-549

    Northern Qi dynasty 550-577

Sui dynasty 581-617

Tang dynasty 618-907

Five Dynasties period 907-960

Liao dynasty 936-1125

Northern Song dynasty 960-1127

Southern Song dynasty 1127-1279

Jin dynasty 1115-1234

Yuan dynasty 1279-1368

Ming dynasty 1368-1644

Qing dynasty 1644-1912

Korean Art

Neolithic, Bronze, Iron Ages 3000-200 BC

Three Kingdoms 57 BC-AD 668

Unified Silla Kingdom 668-918

Koryo period 918-1392

Choson period 1392-1910

Japanese Art

Jomon period 11,000-300 BC

Yayoi period 300 BC-AD 300

Kofun period AD 300-645

Asuka period 552-645

Nara period 645-794

Heian period 794-1185

Kamakura period 1185-1333

Nambokucho period 1333-1392

Muromachi period 1392-1568

Momoyama period 1568-1615

Edo period 1615-1868

Meiji period 1868-1912

Taisho period 1912-1926

Showa period 1926-1989

Heisei period 1989-

The Collection

Fish-Shaped Palette. Mudstone. Egypt, Predynastic (late Naqada I-early Naqada II), ca. 3500 BC. L. 23.3. Bequest of Elizabeth M. Skala. 89.32

Painted Jar. Earthenware. Egypt, Predynastic, ca. 3200 BC. H. 31.4. Gift of the John Huntington Art and Polytechnic Trust. 14.639

Spouted Bowl. Anorthosite gneiss. Egypt, Dynasties IV-V, 2575-2323 BC. W. 14.1. Leonard C. Hanna, Jr., Fund and various donors by exchange. 85.108

Head of King Weserkaf. Limestone. Egypt, Dynasty V, 2465-2458 BC. H. 17.2. Leonard C. Hanna, Jr., Fund. 79.2

Relief from the Tomb of Ny-ankh-nesut. Painted limestone. Egypt, Saqqara, 1st half Dynasty VI, 2323-2255 BC. W. 174. Gift of the John Huntington Art and Polytechnic Trust. 30.736

Statue of Ny-kau-ra, Overseer of the Granary. Red granite. Egypt, Saqqara, 2d half Dynasty V, ca. 2416-2323 BC. H. 54. Leonard C. Hanna, Jr., Fund. 64.90

Panel from the False Door of Ny-kau-ra. Limestone. Egypt, Saqqara, 2d half Dynasty V, ca. 2416-2323 BC. H. 111.8. Leonard C. Hanna, Jr., Fund. 64.91

Amenemhet III. Diabase. Egypt, Dynasty XII, 1844-1797 BC. H. 50.5. Purchase from the J. H. Wade Fund. 60.56

Coffin of Senbi. Painted wood. Egypt, Meir, Dynasty XII, 1991-1783 BC. L. 200.5. Gift of the John Huntington Art and Polytechnic Trust. 14.716

Striding Goat. Limestone with Egyptian blue inlay. Mesopotamia, Sumerian, late 4th millennium BC. W. 3.1. Norman O. Stone and Ella A. Stone Memorial Fund. 84.35

Cup with Procession of Bulls. Basalt. Mesopotamia, Sumerian, probably 3000-2800 BC. D. 7.7. Purchase from the J. H. Wade Fund. 82.1

Recumbent Bull. Basalt. Mesopotamia, Sumerian, ca. 2700 BC. L. 13.6. Purchase from the J. H. Wade Fund. 70.61

Two Seals with a Bull and Unicorn. Steatite. India, Indus Valley period, 3000-1500 BC. Max. H. 3.5. Purchase from the J. H. Wade Fund. 73.160-.161

Jar. Earthenware with slip painting. China, Neolithic period, Yangshao culture, ca. 2500-2000 BC. H. 36.2. The Charles W. Harkness Endowment Fund. 30.332

Gudea, Ensi (Governor) of Lagash. Granodiorite. Mesopotamia, Lagash, Neo-Sumerian, 2141-2122 BC. H. 122.2. Purchase from the J. H. Wade Fund. 63.154

Foundation Nail of Gudea. Copper alloy. Mesopotamia, Neo-Sumerian, ca. 2141-2122 BC. H. 17.8 John L. Severance Fund. 90.31

Storage Vessel. Earthenware. Japan, Middle Jomon period, ca. 2000 BC. H. 61. John L. Severance Fund. 84.68

Hittite Priest-King. Andesite. North Syria, ca. 1600 BC. H. 87.6. Leonard C. Hanna, Jr., Fund. 71.45

Wine Warmer (Jue). Bronze. China, Shang dynasty, Erligang period, 15th c. BC. H. 32.4. John L. Severance Fund. 82.148

Battle Axe, Turned Armilla, and Ingot Torque. Bronze. Hungary, ca. 1500 BC. *Spiral Armilla.* Bronze. Central Europe, ca. 1500 BC. Max. L. 24.2. Purchase from the J. H. Wade Fund. 88.3-.6

Mirror with Handle in the Form of a Nude Girl. Bronze. Egypt, Dynasty XVIII, reign of Tuthmosis III, 1479-1425 BC. H. 38.9. Leonard C. Hanna, Jr., Fund. 83.196

Mirror with Handle in the Form of the God Bes. Bronze. Egypt, Dynasty XVIII, reign of Tuthmosis III, 1479-1425 BC. H. 32.3. Leonard C. Hanna, Jr., Fund. 83.195

Amenhotep III Wearing the "Blue Crown." Granodiorite. Egypt, Dynasty XVIII, ca. 1391-1353 BC. H. 39.3. Gift of the Hanna Fund. 52.513

Head of Amenhotep III. Brown quartzite. Egypt, Dynasty XVIII, ca. 1391-1353 BC. H. 16. Leonard C. Hanna, Jr., Fund. 61.417

Four Nome Gods Bearing Offerings below Fragmentary Scene of Amenhotep III before the God Amen. Painted limestone. Egypt, Thebes, Dynasty XVIII, ca. 1391-1353 BC. W. 132. John L. Severance Fund. 61.205,76.51

Stone Seated Figure. Mexico, Olmec, ca. 1200-600 BC. H. 26. The Norweb Collection. 51.179

Nefertiti Offering to the Aten. Painted sandstone. Egypt, Karnak, Dynasty XVIII, reign of Akhenaten (Amenhotep IV), 1353-1348 BC. L. 43.5. Purchase from the J. H. Wade Fund. 59.186

Ostracon with Ramesses II Being Suckled by a Goddess. Painted limestone. Egypt, Dynasty XIX, reign of Ramesses II, 1290-1224 BC. H. 31.2. Given in honor of James N. Sherwin, Trustee 1957-1971. 87.156

Tomb Relief of the King's Scribe Amenhotep and His Wife Renut. Painted limestone. Egypt, Deir Durunka, Dynasty XIX, 1307-1196 BC. W. 123.1. Leonard C. Hanna, Jr., Fund. 63.100

Coffin Case and Cover of Bekenmut. Wood with gesso and paint. Egypt, Thebes, Dynasty XXI, ca. 1070-945 BC. H. 208.3. Gift of the John Huntington Art and Polytechnic Trust. 14.561

Bronze Stag. Anatolia, Hittite, perhaps 1400-1200 BC or earlier. H. 14. Purchase from the J. H. Wade Fund. 75.13

Axe (Yue). Bronze. China, Shang dynasty, Anyang period, 13th-11th c. BC. H. 21.1. Edward L. Whittemore Fund. 37.27

Dagger-Axe (Ge). Jade (nephrite). China, Shang dynasty, Anyang period, 12th c. BC. L. 18.1. Purchase from the J. H. Wade Fund. 83.2

Fitting. Marble. China, Shang dynasty, Anyang period, 12th c. BC. W. 13.5. Anonymous Gift. 52.585

Ebony Statuette of a Man. Inlaid with glass. Egypt, Dynasty XVIII, reign of Amenhotep III, ca. 1391-1353 BC. H. 23.1. Purchase from the J. H. Wade Fund. 83.98

Ritual Vase with Relief Decoration. Earthenware. Turkey or Syria, Hittite, 1400-1200 BC. H. 61.2. Purchase from the J. H. Wade Fund. 85.70

Wine Beaker (Gu). Bronze. China, Shang dynasty, Anyang period, 12th-11th c. BC. H. 26.8. John L. Severance Fund. 60.43

Food Cauldron (Ding). Bronze. China, Shang dynasty, Anyang period, 11th c. BC. H. 24.5. John L. Severance Fund. 62.281

Grain Steamer (Xian). Bronze. China, Shang dynasty, Anyang period, 11th c. BC. H. 39.4. Purchase from the J. H. Wade Fund. 75.96

Kneeling Priest of Amen. Bronze. Egypt, Dynasty XX, 1196-1070 BC. H. 15.8. John L. Severance Fund. 80.2

Ritual Vessel: "The Bear Lady." Earthenware. Iran, Marlik, ca. 1200-1000 BC. H. 21.5. James Albert and Mary Gardiner Ford Memorial Fund. 67.35

Square Wine Bucket (Fang you). Bronze. China, Shang dynasty, Anyang period, 11th c. BC. H. 26.7. John L. Severance Fund. 63.103

Pendant. Jade (nephrite). China, Western Zhou dynasty, late 11th-mid 10th c. BC. H. 11.2. Gift of Mary B. Lee, C. Bingham Blossom, Dudley S. Blossom III, in memory of Elizabeth B. Blossom. 72.38

Jadeite Seated Figure. Mexico, Olmec, ca. 900-100 BC. H. 11. Purchase from the J. H. Wade Fund. 41.390

Bowl with Incised Decoration. Stone. Peru, North Coast, Chavin, 1st millennium BC. H. 6.5. Purchase from the J. H. Wade Fund. 55.167

Gold Spoon. Peru, North Coast, Chavin, 1st millennium BC. L. 17.5. Gift of Mr. and Mrs. Paul Tishman. 58.177

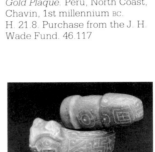

Gold Plaque. Peru, North Coast, Chavin, 1st millennium BC. H. 21.8. Purchase from the J. H. Wade Fund. 46.117

Jadeite Head. Mexico, Olmec, ca. 900-100 BC. H. 7.3. Purchase from the J. H. Wade Fund. 61.31

Stirrup Vessel. Earthenware. Peru, Chavin, 1st millennium BC. H. 22.7. Purchase from Bequest of Helen Humphreys. 68.192

Mortar and Pestle. Stone. Peru, North Coast, Chavin, ca. 1500-100 BC. Pestle: L. 10.7. Mortar: H. 5.7. In memory of Mr. and Mrs. Henry Humphreys, Gift of their daughter, Helen. 57.494

Winged Genie Pollinating Date Palm. Alabaster. Mesopotamia, Nimrud, Assyrian, reign of Ashurnasirpal II, 883-859 BC. H. 249. Purchase from the J. H. Wade Fund. 43.246

Stone Ceremonial Axe. Mexico, Olmec, ca. 900-100 BC. H. 32.1. Gift of the Hanna Fund. 54.856

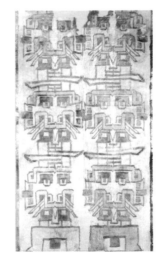

Ritual Cloth. Tabby weave, extended tabby with supplementary weft, warp wrapping; cotton. Peru, Chavin culture, ca. 1000-600 BC. H. 112. John L. Severance Fund. 85.139

Tomb Relief: Mentu-em-het in Ecclesiastical Dress. Limestone. Egypt, late Dynasty XXV-early Dynasty XXVI, ca. 660-650 BC. H. 103.6. Gift of the Hanna Fund. 51.280

Silver Cup with Hunting Scene. Northwestern Iran, said to be from Amlash, late 2d millennium BC. D. 16.5. Purchase from the J. H. Wade Fund. 65.25

Gold Beaker. Northwestern Iran, ca. 1100-1000 BC. H. 14. Purchase from the J. H. Wade Fund. 65.26

Wine Jar (Zun). Bronze. China, Western Zhou dynasty, late 11th-mid 10th c. BC. H. 29.5. Gift from Howard Hollis and Company. 51.151

Wine Jar (Hu). Bronze. China, Western Zhou dynasty, mid 10th-mid 9th c. BC. H. 46.3. Purchase from the J. H. Wade Fund. 44.61

Axe Head. Bronze, cast in bi-part mold. North-Central Caucasus, Kuban culture, ca. 800 BC. L. 18.2. Purchase from the J. H. Wade Fund. 88.2

Plaque: Man and Griffin. Ivory. Iraq, Nimrud, Phoenician, 9th c. BC. H. 6.5. Acquired through contribution of the J. H. Wade Fund from the British School of Archaeology in Iraq. 68.45

"Horse Bit" with Two Winged Ibexes. Bronze. Iran, Luristan, 800-600 BC. W. 23.6. Purchase from the J. H. Wade Fund. 80.102

Votive Pin (detail). Silver. Iran, Luristan, ca. 800-600 BC. D. 15.8. James Parmelee Fund. 63.257

Food Cauldron (Li). Bronze. China, Western Zhou dynasty, mid 10th-mid 9th c. BC. D. 27.1. Gift from Various Donors by Exchange and the John L. Severance Fund. 61.203

Bell (Zhong). Bronze. China, Western Zhou dynasty, mid 9th-early 8th c. BC. H. Leonard C. Hanna, Jr., Fund. 89.3

Ivory Plaque: Crio-Sphinxes. Iraq, Nimrud, Phoenician, 9th c. BC. H. 15.1. Acquired through contribution of the J. H. Wade Fund from the British School of Archaeology in Iraq. 68.47

Beaker. Silver. Iran, Luristan, 9th-7th c. BC. H. 10.2. Gift of K. Rabenou. 63.95

Bull's Head Cauldron Ornament. Bronze. Urartu, 8th-7th c. BC. H. 15.9. Purchase from the J. H. Wade Fund. 42.204

Head of an Ibex. Bronze. Iran, Achaemenian, late 6th-early 5th c. BC. H. 17.2. Gift of Katharine Holden Thayer. 61.199

Grain Steamer with Square Base (Gui). Bronze. China, Eastern Zhou dynasty, Spring and Autumn period, 7th-6th c. BC. H. 34.3. Leonard C. Hanna, Jr., Fund 74.73

Bell (Bo). Bronze. China, Eastern Zhou dynasty, Warring States period, early 5th c. BC. H. 41.3. John L. Severance Fund. 62.44

Peru　　　　　　**Italy**　　　　　　　　　　　　　　　　　**Greece**

Poncho. Needle réseau; wool. Peru, South Coast, Paracas culture, middle period, ca. 600-400 BC. H. 94. The Norweb Collection. 40.514

Warrior. Bronze (lost-wax cast). Sardinia, 9th-8th c. BC. H. 20.2. Leonard C. Hanna, Jr., Fund. 90.1

Krater. Earthenware with slip decoration. Attr. to the Painter of Vatican 88, Greek, Corinthian, ca. 600 BC. D. 52.7. Purchase from the J. H. Wade Fund. 90.81

Figure Vase in the Form of a Heron. Earthenware. Greek, 580-550 BC. H. 13. John L. Severance Fund. 88.65

Fringed Poncho. Embroidery; wool. Peru, South Coast, Paracas culture, late period, ca. 300-100 BC. H. 147.3. The Norweb Collection. 46.227

Dancer or Maenad. Bronze. Italy, Etruscan, late 6th c. BC. H. 18.7. Purchase from the J. H. Wade Fund. 53.124

Satyr Finial from a Kottabos Stand. Bronze. Italy, Etruscan, ca. 470-450 BC. H. 15. Purchase from the J. H. Wade Fund. 74.16

Pawing Bull. Bronze. South Italy, probably Tarentum, 6th-5th c. BC. L. 18.4. Purchase from the J. H. Wade Fund. 30.336

The Atalanta Lekythos. Painted white-ground earthenware. Attr. to Douris, Greek, Athenian, 500-490 BC. H. 31.8. Leonard C. Hanna, Jr., Fund. 66.114

Caryatid Mirror. Bronze. Greek, Sikyon(?), ca. 470-460 BC. H. 38.7. Purchase from the J. H. Wade Fund. 50.7

Fragment of Embroidered Cloth (detail). Embroidery; wool. Peru, South Coast, Paracas culture, late period, ca. 300-100 BC. Overall W. 137.8. The Norweb Collection. 40.528

Cista Handle: Sleep and Death Carrying off the Slain Sarpedon. Bronze. Italy, Etruscan, early 4th c. BC. L. 17.2. Purchase from the J. H. Wade Fund. 45.13

Volute Krater with Departure of Amphiaraos. Red-figure earthenware with added colors. Attr. to the Darius Painter, South Italy, Apulian, 340 BC. H. 103. Leonard C. Hanna, Jr., Fund. 88.41

Bell Krater with Dionysiac Scene. Earthenware with slip decoration. Greek, Athenian, ca. 420-400 BC. D. 40.3 cm. John L. Severance Fund. 89.73

Lekythos with the Birth of Erichthonios. Red-figure earthenware with added gilded relief. Attr. to the Meidias Painter, Greek, Athenian, ca. 410 BC. H. 30.3. Leonard C. Hanna, Jr., Fund. 82.142

Hydria. Black-figure earthenware. Attr. to the Antimenes Painter, Greek, Athenian, ca. 530-510 BC. H. 42.2. Purchase from the J. H. Wade Fund. 75.1

Kouros Torso. Island marble. Greek, 2d quarter 6th c. BC. H. 62.5. Gift of the Hanna Fund. 53.125

Eye Kylix. Red-figure earthenware. Attr. to Psiax, Greek, Athenian, ca. 520 BC. W. 37.6. Purchase from the J. H. Wade Fund. 76.89

Dinos. Black-figure earthenware. Circle of Antimenes Painter, Greek, Athenian, ca. 520-515 BC. Diam. 50.8. John L. Severance Fund. 71.46

Fluted Ring. Jade (nephrite). China, Eastern Zhou dynasty, Warring States period, 5th-4th c. BC. W. 9.1. John L. Severance Fund. 85.75

Finial. Bronze inlaid with silver, gold, and speculum. China, Eastern Zhou dynasty, Warring States period, 4th-3rd c. BC. H. 13.5. Purchase from the J. H. Wade Fund. 30.730

The Cleveland Krater. Earthenware with slip decoration. Attr. to the Cleveland Painter, Greek, Athenian, ca. 470-460 BC. H. 58. Purchase from the J. H. Wade Fund. 30.104

Athlete Making an Offering. Bronze. Greek, probably from workshop of Locri or Tarentum, ca. 450-425 BC. H. 21.2. Gift of the Hanna Fund. 55.684

Mirror Rest: Siren. Bronze with silver inlays. Greek, probably Corinthian, ca. 475 BC. H. 11.4. John L. Severance Fund. 67.204

Hydria. Bronze. Greek, late 5th c. BC. H. 41.6. John L. Severance Fund. 86.23

Wine Jar (Hu). Bronze. China, Eastern Zhou dynasty, Warring States period, 5th c. BC. H. 25.5. Purchase from the J. H. Wade Fund. 75.62

Jar. Ash-glazed stoneware. China, Eastern Zhou dynasty, Warring States period, 3d c. BC. W. 21.5. Edward L. Whittemore Fund. 59.350

Box Mirror with Head of Athena. Bronze. Greek, early 4th c. BC. Diam. 11.3. Leonard C. Hanna, Jr., Fund. 72.66,a

Figure of a Rider. Bronze. Greek (Tarentum, Italy?), ca. 400-375 BC. H. 13.3. Purchase from the J. H. Wade Fund. 77.41

Drum Stand. Lacquered wood. China, Eastern Zhou dynasty, Warring States period, 4th-3d c. BC. H. 132.1. Purchase from the J. H. Wade Fund. 38.9

| **Mexico** | **Costa Rica** | **Greco-Roman World** | **Italy** | | **Egypt** |

Jade Mask. Mexico, Olmec, ca. 300 BC–AD 100. H. 13.7. Gift of Mr. and Mrs. James B. Wadhams in memory of Miss Helen Humphreys. 67.154

Jaguar Macehead. Stone. Costa Rica, Nicoya, 300 BC–AD 300. H. 8.7. In memory of Mr. and Mrs. Henry Humphreys, Gift of their daughter, Helen. 49.469

Hair Ringlets with Ram Heads. Gold. Greek, Hellenistic, ca. 4th c. BC. W. 3.5. Norman O. Stone and Ella A. Stone Memorial Fund. 68.102-.103

Swimming Duck Askos. Earthenware with slip decoration. Italy, Chiusi, Etruscan, 2d half 4th c. BC. L. 25. Purchase from the J. H. Wade Fund. 75.23

Portrait of a Priest or Official. Diabase. Egypt, Dynasty XXX or early Ptolemaic period, 4th c. BC. H. 17.8. John L. Severance Fund. 89.33

Earthenware Seated Figure. Mexico, Oaxaca, Zapotec, Monte-Alban II, ca. 200 BC–AD 200. H. 32.2. Gift of the Hanna Fund. 54.857

Aphrodite Torso. Thasian marble. Greek (Tarentum, Italy), Hellenistic, 2d-1st c. BC. H. 66.3. John L. Severance Fund. 88.9

Lasa. Bronze with silver inlays. Italy, Etruscan, 3d or early 2d c. BC. H. 21.6. Purchase from the J. H. Wade Fund. 47.68

Lekythos: Pan Offering Hare to a Woman. Black-figure earthenware with added colors. South Italy, Campania, 330-300 BC. H. 25.7. John L. Severance Fund. 85.1

Tomb Lintel with Female Musicians. Limestone. Egypt, Memphis(?), Dynasty XXX, 380-343 BC. W. 32.2. Gift of the John Huntington Art and Polytechnic Trust. 14.542

Earthenware Dog. Mexico, Colima, ca. 100 BC–AD 300. H. 39.7. Cornelia Blakemore Warner Fund. 64.37

Stemless Kylix. Silver. Greek, ca. 3d c. BC. W. 17.2 cm. Gift of Mr. and Mrs. Max Ratner. 77.166

Fibula. Gold. South Italy, Campania, 4th-3d c. BC. L. 8.5. John L. Severance Fund. 47.504

Fish Plate. Red-figure earthenware with added colors. South Italy, Paestum, 340-330 BC. D. 38.3. Leonard C. Hanna, Jr., Fund. 85.50

Torso of the General and Prophet, Amen-pa-yom. Granodiorite. Egypt, Ptolemaic period, ca. 280-250 BC. H. 95.3. Gift of the Hanna Fund. 48.141

Temple Relief of a Deity. Limestone. Egypt, Dynasty XXX to early Ptolemaic period, 4th c. BC. H. 47.3. John L. Severance Fund. 72.45

Stag Plaque. Gold. Central Asia, Scythian, 4th c. BC. W. 5.7. The Severance and Greta Millikin Purchase Fund. 85.77

Fertility Ring. Steatite. India, Maurya period, 3d c. BC. D. 10.2. Purchase from the J. H. Wade Fund. 77.36

Finial. Bronze. China, Inner Mongolia, Ordos Steppe region, 4th-2d c. BC. H. 17.8. Edward L. Whittemore Fund. 62.46

Apis Bull. Serpentinite. Egypt, probably early Ptolemaic period, 400-100 BC. L. 58. Leonard C. Hanna, Jr., Fund. 69.118

Shrew. Bronze. Egypt, ca. 600-300 BC. L. 21. Sundry Purchase Fund. 64.358

Elk Fawn. Gold, solid cast. Scythian or Sarmatian(?), 4th-3d c. BC. H. 2.2. Andrew R. and Martha Holden Jennings Fund. 82.2

Section of a Coping Rail. Stone. India, Bharhut, Sunga period, 2d c. BC. W. 122. Gift of Severance and Greta Millikin. 72.366

Standing Horse. Bronze. China, Western Han dynasty, 2d c. BC. H. 6.5. Andrew R. and Martha Holden Jennings Fund. 77.57

Box in the Form of a Composite Capital. Faience. Egypt, Ptolemaic period, 323-30 BC. L. 11.15. Gift of Shelby White; Purchase from the J. H. Wade Fund; and, by exchange, the Gift of the John Huntington Art and Polytechnic Trust. 87.127

Center-Bead and Two Triratna-Shaped Necklace Pendants. Gold repoussé with granulation. India, Sunga period, 2d-1st c. BC. Max. H. 5.7. John L. Severance Fund. 73.66-.68

Head of a Yaksha. Red mottled sandstone. India, Mathura, Sunga period, 1st c. BC. H. 48.2. Norman O. Stone and Ella A. Stone Memorial Fund. 62.45

The Kill. Shell with painting over incised design (one of pair). China, Warring States period or Western Han dynasty, 3d-2d c. BC. W. 8.9. Gift of Mr. and Mrs. Harold T. Clark in memory of Flora L. Terry. 57.139

Furniture Ornament: Head of a Mule. Bronze. Greek, from Kertch, Hellenistic, 2d c. BC. H. 20.4. Purchase from the J. H. Wade Fund. 43.68

Tritoness Relief Appliqué. Bronze with copper inlays. Greek, Hellenistic, late 2d c. BC. W. 24.5. Leonard C. Hanna, Jr., Fund. 85.184

Statuette of a Goat. Bronze. Greek, Hellenistic, 3d-2d c. BC. L. 31.1. Leonard C. Hanna, Jr., Fund. 90.32

Situla. Bronze. Egypt, Armant, probably Ptolemaic period, 304-30 BC. H. 28.2. The Charles W. Harkness Endowment Fund. 32.32

Portrait Bust of a Man. Bronze. Roman, late Republican, 40-30 BC. H. 38.1. Gift of the John Huntington Art and Polytechnic Trust. 28.860

Relief of Apollo and Nike. Greek marble. Roman, Neo-Attic, 1st c. BC. H. 46.4. Purchase from the J. H. Wade Fund. 30.522

Black Street Character. Bronze with silver and copper inlays. Greek, probably Alexandrian, late Hellenistic, ca. 100-50 BC. H. 18.5. Leonard C. Hanna, Jr., Fund. 63.507

Harpocrates. Bronze with silver inlays. Greek, probably Alexandrian, late Hellenistic, ca. 50 BC. H. 27. Purchase from the J. H. Wade Fund. 72.6

Ceremonial Cloth. Tabby weave, painted; cotton. Peru, South Coast, early Nazca Phase 'A,' ca. 1st-3d c. AD. W. 254.2. The Norweb Collection. 40.530

Hercules. Bronze with silver and copper inlays. Roman, early Imperial, ca. 30 BC-AD 20. H. 14.5. Purchase from the J. H. Wade Fund. 87.2

The Vicarello Goblet. Silver. Italy, Vicarello (ancient Aquae Apollinares), early Imperial, late 1st c. BC-early 1st c. AD. H. 11.1. Purchase from the J. H. Wade Fund. 66.371

Funerary Portrait of a Young Girl. Wood with colored, melted wax and gilding. Egypt, Roman period, 2d c. AD. H. 40. John L. Severance Fund. 71.137

Jar (Hu). Painted earthenware. China, Western Han dynasty, late 2d or early 1st c. BC. H. 48.2. The Severance and Greta Millikin Purchase Fund. 89.15

Female Attendant. Earthenware. China, Western Han dynasty, 2d c. BC. H. 54.9. Leonard C. Hanna, Jr., Fund. 83.6

Perfume Askos. Agate and gold. Egypt, Greco-Roman, 1st-2d c. AD. H. 6.5. Andrew R. and Martha Holden Jennings Fund. 64.92

Procession of Nobles. Limestone. Syria, Palmyra, 100-150. L. 120.7. Purchase from the J. H. Wade Fund. 70.15

Pendant with Deity Hariti. Gold and carnelian. India, Gandhara, from Sirkap, ca. 2d c. AD. D. 7.3. Purchase from the J. H. Wade Fund. 53.14

Jar (Hu). Iron-glazed stoneware. China, Eastern Han dynasty, 1st c. AD. H. 45.7. Edward L. Whittemore Fund. 54.370

Dog. Lead-glazed earthenware. China, Eastern Han dynasty, 1st c. AD. H. 36.5. Purchase from the J. H. Wade Fund. 83.1

Maenad and Satyr. Tapestry weave; wool and linen. Egypt, late Roman or early Byzantine period, 2d-4th c. H. 138. Purchase from the J. H. Wade Fund. 75.6

Incense Burner. Bronze. Iran, Parthian, 1st c. AD. L. 30.5. Purchase from the J. H. Wade Fund. 61.32

Tomb Relief. Crystalline limestone. Syria, Palmyra, ca. 230. W. 73.7. Leonard C. Hanna, Jr., Fund. 64.359

Miracle at Sravasti. Gray schist. India, Gandhara, Peshawar area, ca. AD 100. W. 29.2. Andrew R. and Martha Holden Jennings Fund. 75.102

Wall Tile. Stone. China, Eastern Han dynasty, 2d c. L. 166.4. Andrew R. and Martha Holden Jennings Fund. 85.73

Celtic Head. Sandstone.
Northern England(?), 2d-3d c.
H. 33. Gift of Dr. and Mrs. Jacob
Hirsch. 55.555

Youth with Jumping Weights.
Marble. Italy, Roman, mid 1st c.
AD. H. 74.6. Leonard C. Hanna,
Jr., Fund. 85.79

Orestes Sarcophagus. Marble.
Italy, Roman, early 2d c. AD.
L. 209.5. Gift of the John Hunt-
ington Art and Polytechnic
Trust. 28.856

*Group of Marbles: Jonah
Swallowed, Jonah Cast Up,
Jonah Praying, The Good Shep-
herd, and Jonah under the
Gourd Vine*. Eastern Mediterranean, 2d or 3d c. Max. H.
51.6. John L. Severance Fund.
65.237-.241

Portrait of a Man. Crystalline
island marble. Eastern Roman
Empire, ca. AD 161-169. H. 38.2.
Purchase from the J. H. Wade
Fund. 52.260

*Emperor, Probably Marcus
Aurelius (r. 161-180), as
Philosopher*. Bronze. Roman,
late 2d c. AD. H. 193. Leonard C.
Hanna, Jr., Fund. 86.5

*Oil Ampulla in the Form of a
Dancing Bear*. Bronze. Roman,
3d c. AD. H. 14.6. Purchase from
the J. H. Wade Fund. 72.102

*Portrait of the Emperor
Balbinus*. Marble. Italy, Roman,
ca. AD 238. H. 18.5. Gift from
J. H. Wade. 25.945

Portrait Bust of a Man. Marble.
Eastern Mediterranean, 3d c.
H. 33.8. John L. Severance
Fund. 65.247

Stair-Riser with a Bacchanalian Scene. Schist. India, Gandhara, from Buner, 1st c. AD. W. 43.2. Dudley P. Allen Fund. 30.329

Standing Sakyamuni. Gray schist. India, Gandhara, prob. Peshawar, 2d half 2d c. H. 119.7. Gift of Morris and Eleanor Everett in memory of Flora Morris Everett. 72.43

Bodhisattva. Gray schist. India, Gandhara, late 2d c. H. 132.4. Purchase from the J. H. Wade Fund. 65.476

Fowling Tower. Lead-glazed earthenware. China, Eastern Han dynasty, 1st-2d c. H. 54.3. The Severance and Greta Millikin Purchase Fund. 89.71

Dotaku: Ceremonial Object. Japan, Yayoi period, ca. 100-300. H. 97.8. Gift of Mrs. Arthur St. John Newberry. 16.1102

Seated Buddha. Gray schist. India, Gandhara, 3d c. H. 129.5. Leonard C. Hanna, Jr., Fund. 61.418

Attendant Bearing a Fly-Whisk (Chauri). Red sandstone. India, Mathura, Kushan period, early 2d c. H. 55.8. Andrew R. and Martha Holden Jennings Fund. 65.472

Nagini. Red mottled sandstone. India, Mathura, Kushan period, 1st-2d c. H. 124.4. Purchase from the J. H. Wade Fund. 68.104

Seated Sakyamuni. Red mottled sandstone. India, Mathura, Kushan period, late 1st-early 2d c. H. 51.4. Purchase from the J. H. Wade Fund. 70.63

Tomb Door. Sandstone. China, Eastern Han dynasty, 1st-2d c. H. 120. John L. Severance Fund. 62.280

Ladies Entertained by Dancers. Ivory. India, Begram, Kushan period, 1st-2d c. L. 17. Leonard C. Hanna, Jr., Fund. 85.103

Torana Bracket with Salabhanjika Figures. Red sandstone. India, Mathura, Kushan period, 2d half 2d c. H. 71.1. John L. Severance Fund. 71.15

Nagaraja. Red mottled sandstone. India, Mathura, Kushan period, 3d c. H. 67.3. Purchase from the J. H. Wade Fund. 43.661

Mirror. Bronze. China, Eastern Han dynasty, 2d c. D. 20.9. The Severance and Greta Millikin Purchase Fund. 89.102

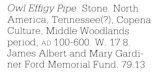

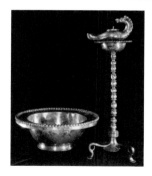

Owl Effigy Pipe. Stone. North America, Tennessee(?), Copena Culture, Middle Woodlands period, AD 100-600. W. 17.8. James Albert and Mary Gardiner Ford Memorial Fund. 79.13

The Nereid. Tapestry weave; wool and linen. Egypt, Byzantine period, late 4th-early 5th c. H. 66.5. Purchase from the J. H. Wade Fund. 53.18

Tigress and Cubs. Stone mosaic. Eastern Roman Empire, 4th c. L. 142.9. John L. Severance Fund. 87.65

Spoon. Silver with partial gilding and niello inscription. Byzantium, mid 4th c. L. 12.5. John L. Severance Fund. 64.39

Bowl and Lamp. Silver. Byzantium, late 4th c. D. 27.8, H. 48.6 resp. Purchase from the J. H. Wade Fund. 54.259/54.597

Rhyton in Form of a Horse. Silver, gilt. Iran, Sasanian, 3d-early 4th c. L. 33.7. John L. Severance Fund. 64.41

Dancing Pan. Limestone. Egypt, Coptic period, 4th-5th c. H. 34. John L. Severance Fund. 55.68

Altar Frontal. From the Church of S. Carlino, Ravenna. Marble. Byzantium, Constantinople, early 6th c. W. 169.5. John L. Severance Fund. 48.25

Bowl. Silver and niello. Byzantium, Syria(?), 2d half 4th c. D. 18.5. Purchase from the J. H. Wade Fund. 56.30

Bust of an Empress. Bronze. Byzantium, Theodosian period, late 4th c. H. 10.2. John L. Severance Fund. 67.28

Plate with Royal Hunting Scene. Silver, partially gilt. Iran, Sasanian, 5th or 6th c. D. 20.6. John L. Severance Fund. 62.150

Lunette. Limestone. Egypt, Coptic period, 5th c. W. 61. John L. Severance Fund. 55.63

Vase. Silver with traces of gilding. Byzantium, Syria(?), late 4th-6th c. H. 40. Purchase from the J. H. Wade Fund with the addition of a gift from Helen Wade Greene. 57.497

Adam and Eve. Mosaic. Byzantium, North Syria, 5th c. H. 142.8. John L. Severance Fund. 69.115

Plate with Goddess Anahita. Silver, partially gilt. Iran, Sasanian period, ca. 6th c. D. 21. John L. Severance Fund. 62.295

Adoration of the Bodhi Tree. Limestone. India, Amaravati, Andhra period, 2d c. AD. H. 80. Purchase from the J. H. Wade Fund. 70.43

Fire Pillar. Limestone. India, Nagarjunakonda, Andhra period, late 2d-early 3d c. H. 59.1. Purchase from the J. H. Wade Fund. 43.72

Railing Pillar. Sikri sandstone. India, Mathura, Kushan period, 2d c. AD. H. 80. John L. Severance Fund. 77.34

Seated Buddha. Red mottled sandstone. India, Mathura, Kushan period, 3d c. H. 64. Edward L. Whittemore Fund. 41.94

Spirit Jar: Proto-yue Ware. Glazed stoneware. China, Three Kingdoms period, Western Jin dynasty, late 3d c. The Severance and Greta Millikin Purchase Fund. 88.21

Seated Buddha. Red sandstone. India, Mathura, Gupta period, 5th c. H. 82. Leonard C. Hanna, Jr., Fund. 73.214

Seated Ascetics. Terracotta plaque. Kashmir, Harwan, 4th c. H. 40.8. Edward L. Whittemore Fund. 59.132

Head of Bodhisattva Avalokitesvara. Stucco. India, Gandhara, ca. 4th-5th c. H. 45.7. John L. Severance Fund. 85.31

Head of Buddha. Red mottled sandstone. India, Mathura, Gupta period, 5th c. H. 30.5. John L. Severance Fund. 63.504

Votive Stupa. Steatite, dated 435. China, Northern Liang dynasty. H. 16.9. Purchase from the J. H. Wade Fund. 90.84

Vessel. Earthenware. Japan, Yayoi period, ca. 300. H. 34. Edward L. Whittemore Fund. 89.69

Adoring Attendant. Stucco. India, Gandhara, 4th-5th c. H. 54.6. Purchase from the J. H. Wade Fund. 43.395

Standing Buddha. Cream sandstone. India, Sarnath, Gupta period, 5th c. H. 76.2. Purchase from the J. H. Wade Fund. 43.278

Newborn Buddha. Gilt bronze. China, Six Dynasties period, 5th c. H. 19.4. Purchase from the J. H. Wade Fund. 55.46

Haniwa Figure of a Man. Earthenware. Japan, Kofun period, ca. 6th c. H. 58.4. James Parmelee Fund by exchange. 62.39

Mexico | **Andes** | **Egypt** | **Byzantium**

Fragment of a Painted Wall.
Fresco. Mexico, Tlacuilapaxco,
Teotihuacan, ca. 600-750.
W. 116.2. Purchase from the
J. H. Wade Fund. 63.252

Gold Mask. Peru, Moche, ca.
100-500. W. 38.7. In memory of
Mr. and Mrs. Henry Humphreys,
Gift of their daughter, Helen.
56.85

Fragment of a Large Hanging
(detail). Tapestry weave; wool.
Egypt, Antinoë, Byzantine
period, 6th c. Overall W. 158.
Purchase from the J. H. Wade
Fund. 61.201

Pyx. Ivory. Byzantium, 6th c.
H. 8.4. Purchase from the J. H.
Wade Fund. 51.114

Rouge Pot. Glass, sapphire, gold
filigree. Byzantium, 6th c. H. 3.7.
Grace Rainey Rogers Fund.
46.427

Kero. Earthenware. Bolivia,
Highland Tiahuanaco, ca. 300-
600. H. 20.7. John L. Severance
Fund. 63.476

Fragment of a Hanging.
Tapestry weave; wool and linen.
Egypt, Antinoë, Byzantine
period, late 6th c. H. 76 2.
Purchase from the J. H. Wade
Fund. 80.31

Necklace with Pendants. Gold
with garnet. Byzantium, 6th c.
L. of chain 45.7. Dudley P. Allen
Fund, Elisabeth Severance
Prentiss Fund. 46.260

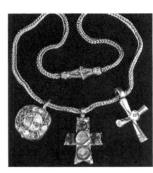

Chain with Pendants. Gold,
enamel, and glass. Byzantium,
probably Syria, early 6th c. L. of
chain 31.5. Purchase from the
J. H. Wade Fund. 47.35

Fragmentary Hanging. Tapestry
inwoven in tabby ground; wool
and linen. Egypt, Byzantine
period, 6th c. H. 105.4. John L.
Severance Fund. 82.73

Portrait Intaglio. Gold, filigree,
and amethyst. Byzantium, 6th c.
H. 3.3. Purchase from the J. H.
Wade Fund. 47.33

Monogram of Christ. Gold with
garnets. Byzantium, Syria, 6th-
7th c. H. 15. Gift of Lillian M.
Kern. 65.551

Wine Vessel with Figures of the Goddess Anahita. Silver, partially gilt. Iran, Sasanian, 4th-5th c. H. 17.7. Gift of Katharine Holden Thayer. 62.294

Plate with Figures. Silver alloy. India, Gupta period, ca. 5th c. D. 18.8. Purchase from the J. H. Wade Fund. 72.71

Head of Vishnu. Gray sandstone. India, Besnagar, Madhya Pradesh, Gupta period, 4th c. H. 40.6. John L. Severance Fund. 69.57

Stele with Maitreya and Attendants. Sandstone, dated 500. China, Six Dynasties period, Northern Wei dynasty. H. 94.6. Gift of Severance and Greta Millikin. 59.130

Caparisoned Horse. Painted earthenware. China, Six Dynasties period, Northern Wei dynasty, early 6th c. H. 22.2. The Charles W. Harkness Endowment Fund. 29.985

Sakyamuni Buddha. Stone. Korea, Three Kingdoms period, 6th-7th c. H. 11.4. John L. Severance Fund. 87.188

Textile. Compound twill weave; silk. Iran, Sasanian period, 6th-early 7th c. W. 11.4. Gift of The Textile Arts Club. 51.88

Standing Buddha. Bronze, dated 591. India, Gupta period. H. 46. Purchase from the J. H. Wade Fund. 68.40

Vishnu. Buff-colored sandstone. India, possibly Allahabad region, Gupta period, late 5th c. H. 85.4. Purchase from the J. H. Wade Fund. 76.75

Stele with Sakyamuni and Attendants. Limestone, dated 537. China, Six Dynasties period, Eastern Wei dynasty. H. 77.5. Gift of the John Huntington Art and Polytechnic Trust. 14.567

Ring Mount. Gilt bronze. China, Six Dynasties period, 6th c. W. 20. Purchase from the J. H. Wade Fund. 30.731

Textile. Tapestry weave; wool and linen. Iran, Sasanian period, late 6th-early 7th c. W. 24.8. John L. Severance Fund. 50.509

Mithuna: Amorous Couple. Terracotta. India, Ahichchhatra, Uttar Pradesh, Gupta period, 5th-6th c. H. 38.5. Purchase from the J. H. Wade Fund. 71.133

Head of Vishnu. Red mottled sandstone. India, Mathura, Gupta period, 5th c. H. 28. Edward L. Whittemore Fund. 42.498

Stele with Maitreya as the Future Buddha. Marble. China, Six Dynasties period, Northern Qi dynasty, 550-577. H. 86.3. The Worchester R. Warner Collection. 17.320

Caryatid. Stone. China, Six Dynasties period, Northern Qi dynasty, 550-577. W. 40. Anonymous Gift. 57.357

20

Gold Plaque. Panama, Coclé, ca. 500-1000. H. 25.6. Gift of Mrs. R. Henry Norweb, Mrs. Albert S. Ingalls, John L. Severance Fund. 52.459

Mosaic Relief. Peru, Huari, ca. 500-800. H. 6.5. In memory of Mr. and Mrs. Henry Humphreys, Gift of their daughter, Helen. 44.291

Fibula. Silver with garnets. Frankish, 6th c. L. 11. Andrew R. and Martha Holden Jennings Fund. 75.109

Fibula. Silver gilt with garnets. Ostrogothic, early 6th c. L. 13.3. Andrew R. and Martha Holden Jennings Fund. 75.108

Pair of Earrings. Gold with garnets. Ostrogothic, 5th c. Max. D. 3.3. Gift of Dr. and Mrs. John R. McKay. 75.48,a

Scenes from the Old and New Testament. Tabby weave, resist-dyed; linen. Egypt, Byzantine period, 1st half 6th c. H. 104. John L. Severance Fund. 51.400

Icon of the Virgin. Tapestry weave; wool. Egypt, Byzantine period, 6th c. H. 178. Leonard C. Hanna, Jr., Bequest. 67.144

Chalice. From the Beth Misona Treasure. Silver. Byzantium, Syria, 6th-7th c. H. 17.4. Purchase from the J. H. Wade Fund. 50.378

Paten Dedicated to St. Sergius. From the Beth Misona Treasure. Silver. Byzantium, Syria. 6th c. D. 32.2. Purchase from the J. H. Wade Fund. 50.38

Fragment of a Hanging: The Piping Maenad. Looped-knot pile; wool and linen. Egypt, Byzantine period, 6th c. H. 83.5. Gift of The Textile Arts Club. 68.74

Ewer (Jiaodou). Bronze. China, Six Dynasties period, 6th c. H. 22.8. Purchase from the J. H. Wade Fund. 83.214

Coffin Platform (detail): *Phoenix*. Limestone. China, Six Dynasties period, Northern Qi dynasty, 550-577. H. (detail) 45.7. Gift of Mr. and Mrs. Oscar Lange. 82.260

Matrika. Grayish-green schist. India, Tanesara, Rajasthan, Gupta period, early 6th c. H. 73.4. Purchase from the J. H. Wade Fund. 70.12

Vishnu. Red sandstone. India, Mathura, late Gupta period, end 6th c. H. 109.2. John L. Severance Fund. 63.580

Krishna Govardhana. Gray limestone. Cambodia, Phnom Da, Pre-Angkorean period, 1st half 6th c. H. 118.8. John L. Severance Fund. 73.106

Ananda. Limestone. China, Six Dynasties period, Northern Qi dynasty, 550-577. H. 114.5. Leonard C. Hanna, Jr., Fund. 72.166

Mirror. Bronze. China, Sui dynasty, 581-617. D. 14.5. Dudley P. Allen Fund. 26.249

River Goddess Ganga. Buff red-veined sandstone. India, Mathura region, early Medieval period, early 7th c. H. 108. John L. Severance Fund. 66.119

Guanyin. Painted sandstone. China, Six Dynasties period, Northern Qi or early Sui dynasty, late 6th c. H. 138.8. John L. Severance Fund. 62.162

Sakyamuni. Limestone. China, Sui dynasty, 581-617. H. 51.4. John L. Severance Fund. 64.152

Terracotta Head. Mexico, Classic Veracruz style, 5th-9th c. H. 28.7. Purchase from the J. H. Wade Fund. 40.11

Eccentric Flint in Human Shape. Stone. Guatemala, Quirigua, Maya, 6th-8th c. H. 34.6. John L. Severance Fund. 50.161

Rhyton: The Buffalo-Slayer Goddess. Silver, partially gilt, inlaid. Iran, ca. 7th c. H. 19.4. Leonard C. Hanna, Jr., Fund. 64.96

Vishnu Riding on Garuda. Black chlorite. East India, early Pala period, 7th c. H. 81.3. Purchase from the J. H. Wade Fund. 61.46

Three Vessels. Silver with gilding, inscribed. Tibet, mid 7th c. *Beaker:* H. 10.2. The Severance and Greta Millikin Purchase Fund. 88.68. *Rhyton:* H. 30.5. Gift of Mrs. Clara Taplin Rankin. 88.69. *Vase:* H. 22.9. Purchase from the J. H. Wade Fund. 88.67

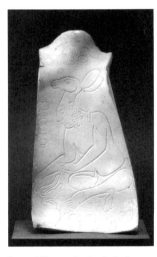

Seated Figure. Incised shell. Mexico or Guatemala, Maya, ca. 600-800. H. 16.5. The Norweb Collection. 65.550

Mukhalinga. Black chlorite. East India, early Pala period, 7th c. H. 83.8. John L. Severance Fund. 73.73

Chakrapurusa: Personification of Vishnu's Wheel. Black chlorite. East India, Apshad, early Pala period, ca. 670. H. 76.8. Purchase from the J. H. Wade Fund. 45.367

Head of a Female. Sandstone. Thailand, Si Thep, 1st half 7th c. H. 26. John L. Severance Fund. 70.11

Ganesha. Limestone. Cambodia, Pre-Angkorean period, 7th c. H. 122. Leonard C. Hanna, Jr., Fund. 87.147

Cylindrical Box with Lid (Lian). Gilt bronze with chased design. China, Tang dynasty, early 7th c. H. 17.2. Leonard C. Hanna, Jr., Fund. 72.44

Candlestand. Glazed stoneware. China, Tang dynasty, 7th c. H. 29.8. The Charles W. Harkness Endowment Fund. 30.322

Guardian Lion. Marble. China, Tang dynasty, 7th c. H. 78.7. Purchase from the J. H. Wade Fund. 65.473

Miroku (The Future Buddha) in Meditation. Bronze. Japan, Asuka period, 7th c. H. 39.4. John L. Severance Fund. 50.86

Head of Buddha. Bluish-gray sandstone. Cambodia, probably from Angkor Borei, Pre-Angkorean period, 7th c. H. 25.4. Dudley P. Allen Fund. 32.43

Eleven-Headed Guanyin. Sandstone. China, Tang dynasty, 1st quarter 8th c. H. 129.5. Gift of Severance and Greta Millikin. 59.129

Bodhisattva. Limestone with traces of pigment. China, Tang dynasty, early 8th c. H. 34.2. Leonard C. Hanna, Jr., Fund. 83.76

Standing Buddha. Sandstone. Thailand, Mon-Dvaravati period, 2d half 7th c. H. 135.3. Leonard C. Hanna, Jr., Fund. 73.15

Eleven-Headed Guanyin. Wood. China, Tang dynasty, late 7th c. H. 62.8. John L. Severance Fund. 70.66

Bodhisattva Kannon. Gilt bronze. Japan, Nara period, 645-710. H. 33. John L. Severance Fund. 50.392

Votive Plaque with Vishnu. Gold repoussé. Thailand, Si Thep, 7th-8th c. H. 7.6. John L. Severance Fund. 73.75

Mesoamerica   **Germany**   **Syria**   **Kashmir**

Woman in Ceremonial Robes. Limestone relief. Mexico or Guatemala, Usumacinta region, Maya, ca. 600–800. W. 69.9. Purchase from the J. H. Wade Fund. 62.32

Jade Head. Honduras, Copan, Maya, 7th–8th c. H. 7.6. Gift of Mrs. R. Henry Norweb, in memory of her Aunt, Delia Holden White. 47.176

Medallion with the Bust of Christ. From the Guelph Treasure. Cloisonné enamel on copper. Germany, Weserraum, late 8th c. D. 5. Purchase from the J. H. Wade Fund. 30.504

Square Ornament from a Tunic. Compound twill weave; silk. Syria, Umayyad period, 8th c. H. 23.5. Purchase from the J. H. Wade Fund. 47.192

Standing Mahadeva. Gray schist. Kashmir, 8th c. H. 53. Bequest of Mrs. Severance A. Millikin. 89.369

Temptation of Buddha by the Evil Forces of Mara. Ivory. Kashmir, 8th c. H. 13. Purchase from the J. H. Wade Fund. 71.18

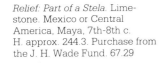

Jadeite Pendant. Mexico or Central America, Maya, 6th–8th c. H. 6.8. John L. Severance Fund. 52.119

Seated Vajrapani: Thunderbolt-Bearer. Brass. Kashmir, 8th c. H. 22.2. Purchase from the J. H. Wade Fund. 71.14

Emaciated Buddha. Ivory. Kashmir. 8th c. H. 12.4. Leonard C. Hanna, Jr., Fund. 86.70

Relief: Part of a Stela. Limestone. Mexico or Central America, Maya, 7th–8th c. H. approx. 244.3. Purchase from the J. H. Wade Fund. 67.29

Tenoned Head. Stone. Honduras, Copan, Maya, 7th–8th c. H. 52.7. Gift of the Hanna Fund. 53.154

Surya, the Sun God. Brass. Kashmir, 8th c. H. 50.3. Gift of Katharine Holden Thayer. 65.557

Female Attendants Bearing Fly-Whisks (Chauri). Ivory. Kashmir, 8th c. H. 7.5. John L. Severance Fund. 72.35–.36

Mirror. Bronze with silver and gold inlaid lacquer. China, Tang dynasty, early 8th c. D. 19.2. Leonard C. Hanna, Jr., Fund. 73.74

Three-Legged Dish. Beaten silver with parcel gilding. China, Tang dynasty, early 8th c. D. 30.5. Leonard C. Hanna, Jr., Fund. 72.39

Stem Cup. Beaten silver with parcel gilding. China, Tang dynasty, early 8th c. H. 8.9. Edward L. Whittemore Fund. 51.396

Woman from an Audience Scene. Unfired clay with color. Japan, early Nara period, 645-710. H. 19. Edward L. Whittemore Fund. 50.393

Devi. Gilt copper. Nepal, 7th-8th c. H. 15.5. Gift of George P. Bickford. 83.153

Vishnu. Gray sandstone. Cambodia, Pre-Angkorean period, style of Prasat Andet, 2d half 7th c. H. 87. Gift of the Hanna Fund. 42.562

Camel. Lead-glazed earthenware. China, Tang dynasty, late 7th-early 8th c. H. 80. John L. Severance Fund. 67.147

Ewer. Lead-glazed earthenware. China, Tang dynasty, early 8th c. H. 27.3. The Severance and Greta Millikin Purchase Fund. 87.148

Ewer. Iron-glazed stoneware. China, Tang dynasty, early 8th c. H. 42.1. John L. Severance Fund. 89.2

Suikoju: Gigaku Mask. Wood (paulownia), lacquered and painted. Japan, Nara period, 710-784. H. 28. John L. Severance Fund. 49.158

Bodhisattva Vajrapani. Gilt copper. Nepal, 8th c. H. 17.8. John L. Severance Fund. 82.52

Maitreya: The Buddha of the Future. Bronze, Cambodia, Pre-Angkorean period, 7th c. H. 28. John L. Severance Fund. 72.7

Woman Holding Plum Blossoms. Earthenware with slip and traces of pigment. China, Tang dynasty, early 8th c. H. 43.8. John L. Severance Fund. 87.13

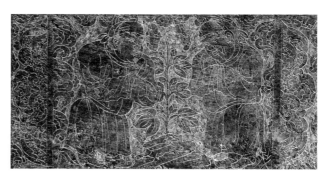

Sarcophagus Panel (detail). Limestone. China, Tang dynasty, early 8th c. Overall H. 119.4. John L. Severance Fund. 75.63

26

Plaque. Crystalline green stone. Mexico or Central America, Maya, 7th-9th c. H. 4.8. In memory of Mr. and Mrs. Henry Humphreys, Gift of their daughter, Helen. 50.153

Incense Burner. Terracotta. Mexico, Palenque region, Maya, 7th-8th c. H. 104.1. Purchase from the J. H. Wade Fund. 65.248

Square Hat. Net work with and without pile; wool. Peru, South Coast, Huari culture, Middle Horizon, ca. 700-1100. H. 14.3. Purchase from the J. H. Wade Fund. 45.378

Poncho. Tapestry weave; wool and cotton. Peru, South Coast, Huari culture, Middle Horizon, ca. 700-1100. W. 115. Gift of William R. Carlisle. 56.84

Textile. Tapestry weave; wool and cotton. Peru, South Coast, Huari culture, Middle Horizon, ca. 700-1100. H. 39.4. Gift of John Wise in memory of Leonard C. Hanna, Jr. 57.495

Sleeve Band. Tapestry inwoven in tabby ground; wool and linen. Egypt, Abbasid period, 2d half 8th c. H. 18.2. Andrew R. and Martha Holden Jennings Fund. 82.107

Tunic Ornament. Tapestry weave; wool and linen. Egypt, Abbasid period, 2d half 8th c. H. 23.3. The A. W. Ellenberger, Sr., Endowment Fund. 69.38

Textile Panel. Tapestry weave; wool and linen. Egypt, al-Bahnasá, Abbasid period, 1st half 9th c. W. 80.5. Purchase from the J. H. Wade Fund. 59.48

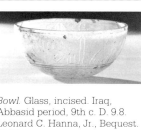

Bowl. Glass, incised. Iraq, Abbasid period, 9th c. D. 9.8. Leonard C. Hanna, Jr., Bequest. 85.21

Ravana Shaking Mount Kailasa. Sandstone. Central India, 8th c. H. 139. Sundry Purchase Fund. 71.173

Stele with the Twenty-Third Jain Tirthankara, Parsvanatha. Sandstone. Central India, 9th c. H. 160.7. John L. Severance Fund. 61.419

Eleven-Headed Avalokitesvara. Brass. Kashmir, 9th c. H. 39.4. Andrew R. and Martha Holden Jennings Fund. 75.101

Buddha Seated in the European Manner. Gilt bronze. Thailand/Burma, ca. 8th-9th c. H. 55.2. Leonard C. Hanna, Jr., Fund. 89.49

Head of Buddha. Volcanic stone. Java, from Borobudur, early 9th c. H. 30.5. Purchase from the J. H. Wade Fund. 42.1087

Bodhisattva. Hollow lacquer with traces of cut gold. China, Tang dynasty, ca. 800. H. 44. Given in memory of Howard Parmelee Eells, Jr., by his wife, Adele Chisholm Eells. 83.86

Textile. Lampas weave; silk. China, Tang Dynasty, 618-907. H. 15.9. Gift of the Norweb Foundation. 57.138

Covered Bowl. Glazed stoneware with stamped designs. Korea, Unified Silla period, 8th-9th c. D. 12. Gift of John L. Severance. 28.178

Plaque: Amitabha Trinity. Embossed copper covered with gold leaf. Korea, Unified Silla period, 668-935. H. 11.5. Purchase from the J. H. Wade Fund. 87.59

Door Guardian, Mahakala. Volcanic stone. Java, from Candi Suko, Boyolali, near Surakarta, ca. 9th c. H. 61.3. Gift of Dr. Norman Zaworski. 80.203

Guanyin. Marble. China, Tang dynasty, 9th c. H. 177.8. Purchase from the J. H. Wade Fund. 29.981

Sakyamuni Attended by Manjusri and Samantabhadra. Hanging scroll, color on silk. China, Tang dynasty, ca. 900. H. 94. Mr. and Mrs. William H. Marlatt Fund. 75.92

Reclining Lion-Dog. Gilt bronze. Korea, Koryo period, 10th c. L. 8.5. Gift of Robert H. Ellsworth in honor of Sherman E. Lee. 87.160

Standing Buddha. Gilt bronze. Korea, Unified Silla period, late 8th c. H. 25.4. Leonard C. Hanna, Jr., Fund. 88.34

Mesoamerica	Germany	Egypt	Byzantium	India	

Fragment of a Clavus: St. George. Embroidery; silk on linen. Egypt, Tulunid period, 9th c. H. 10. Purchase from the J. H. Wade Fund. 48.115

St. George of Cappadocia. Quartz. Byzantium, 10th c. H. 3. Dudley P. Allen Fund. 59.41

Buddha Calling on the Earth to Witness. Black chlorite. East India, Pala period, 9th c. H. 94. Dudley P. Allen Fund. 35.146

The Birth of Buddha. Black chlorite. East India, Pala period, 9th c. H. 46.5. John L. Severance Fund. 59.349

Palma Stone. Gray volcanic stone. Mexico, Classic Veracruz style, ca. 600-900. H. 49.2. Purchase from the J. H. Wade Fund. 73.3

Plaque from a Bookcover: Christ's Mission to the Apostles. Ivory. Germany, Ottonian, ca. 970. H. 18.3. Gift of the John Huntington Art and Polytechnic Trust. 67.65

Stone Yoke. Serpentine with traces of cinnabar. Mexico, Classic Veracruz style, ca. 600-900. H. 42.5. Leonard C. Hanna, Jr., Fund. 73.213

Pottery Bowl. Luster ware. Egypt, Fustat, Fatimid period, 11th c. D. 25.4. Purchase from the J. H. Wade Fund. 44.476

Pendant. From Aachen Cathedral Treasury. Relief: steatite. Byzantium, 10th c. Frame: gilt silver and pearls. France, 2d half 14th c. H. 6.7. Purchase from the J. H. Wade Fund. 51.445

Akshobhya: The Buddha of the East. Bronze. East India, Kurkihar, Bihar, Pala period, 9th c. H. 39.3. Purchase from the J. H. Wade Fund. 70.10

Umamahesvara: Siva and Parvati. Bronze. East India, Pala period, reign of Devapala, 815-854. H. 17.8. John L. Severance Fund. 64.50

Title Page of Abbot Berno's "Tonarius." Ink, tempera, and gold on parchment. Germany, Reichenau, ca. 1020-30. H. 21.4. Purchase from the J. H. Wade Fund. 52.88

Pyx: Christ, The Twelve Apostles, and The Virgin Orans. Ivory. Byzantium, late 10th-early 11th c. H. 9.5. Purchase from the J. H. Wade Fund. 73.4

Lintel with Garuda. Sandstone. Cambodia, Preah Ko style, late 9th c. W. 118. John L. Severance Fund. 67.37

Siva. Sandstone. Vietnam, Ancient Champa, from Dong-duong, 9th c. H. 86.3. Edward L. Whittemore Fund. 35.147

Water and Moon Guanyin. Loquat wood. China, Five Dynasties period, 10th c. H. 15.1. Gift of Mrs. A. Dean Perry. 65.556

Nikko: The Sun Bodhisattva. Wood (Japanese yew). Japan, Heian period, ca. 800. H. 46.7. John L. Severance Fund. 61.48

Standing Buddha. Brass. Kashmir, ca. 10th c. H. 98.1. John L. Severance Fund. 66.30

Torso of a Female Deity. Sandstone. Cambodia, Bakheng style, late 9th-early 10th c. H. 88.9. Purchase from the J. H. Wade Fund. 71.134

Standing Ashura. Bronze. Cambodia, Koh Ker style, 2d quarter of 10th c. H. 17.7. Gift of George P. Bickford. 72.221

Elephant. Beige sandstone. Vietnam, Ancient Champa, Tra-kieu style, 1st half 10th c. H. 58. Purchase from the J. H. Wade Fund. 82.10

Phoenix-Headed Ewer: Qingbai Ware. Glazed porcelain. China, Five Dynasties period or Northern Song dynasty, 10th c. H. 38.7. Gift of Severance and Greta Millikin. 65.468

Seated Shaka. Wood with lacquer and traces of color. Japan, Heian period, ca. 900. H. 57.1. Leonard C. Hanna, Jr., Fund. 86.7

Rakshasa. Gray sandstone. Cambodia, Koh Ker style, 2d quarter 10th c. H. 70. John L. Severance Fund. 67.146

Hanuman. Buff sandstone. Cambodia, Koh Ker style, 2d quarter 10th c. H. 109.9. Leonard C. Hanna, Jr., Fund. 82.46

Amitabha. Gilt bronze. China, Liao dynasty, 10th c. H. 22.8. Purchase from the J. H. Wade Fund. 42.1082

30

Figure of a Warrior. Terracotta. Mexico, Yucatan, Island of Guaymil, Maya, 8th-9th c. H. 26.1. James Albert and Mary Gardiner Ford Memorial Fund. 63.93

Front of a Litter. Painted wood. Peru, North Coast, Lambayeque, ca. 850-1100. H. 57.8. John L. Severance Fund. 52.233

Gold Ewer. Repoussé and engraved gold. Iran, Buyid period, reign of Samsam al-Dawla, 985-998. H. 12.1. Purchase from the J. H. Wade Fund. 66.22

K'o-ssu. Tapestry weave; silk and gold. Central Asia, Chinese Turkestan, 10th(?) c. H. 58. Leonard C. Hanna, Jr., Fund. 88.100

Vaishnava Trinity. Granite. South India, Chola period, 1st half 10th c. *Vishnu*: H. 175.9. John L. Severance Fund. 63.104-.106

Vase. Earthenware with painted decorations. Guatemala, Kixpec, Maya, 8th-9th c. H. 16.5. John L. Severance Fund and Anonymous Gift. 54.391

Panel. Tapestry weave; cotton and wool. Peru, North Coast, Chimu, ca. 1100. H. 88. Purchase from the J. H. Wade Fund. 85.7

Pottery Bowl. Polychrome painted ware. Iran, Nishapur, Samanid period, 10th c. D. 28. Purchase from the J. H. Wade Fund. 56.225

Pottery Bowl. Polychrome painted ware. Iran, Nishapur, Samanid period, 10th c. D. 35.6. Purchase from the J. H. Wade Fund. 59.249

Dragon K'o-ssu. Tapestry weave; silk and gold. Central Asia, Chinese Turkestan, 11th-12th c. H. 59. Andrew R. and Martha Holden Jennings Fund. 88.33

Gajasura-Samharamurti: Siva Killing Elephant Demon. Granite. South India, Chola period, 11th c. H. 72.4. John L. Severance Fund. 62.164

Parvati. Bronze. South India, Chola period, 10th c. H. 64.1. Leonard C. Hanna, Jr., Fund. 84.2

Uma-Sahitamurti: Siva and Parvati. Bronze. South India, Chola period, early 10th c. H. 103.5. John L. Severance Fund. 61.94

Vinadharamurti: Siva as King of Music. Bronze. South India, Chola period, ca. 1000. H. 76. Leonard C. Hanna, Jr., Fund. 71.117

Padmapani: Lotus-Bearing Bodhisattva. Bronze inlaid with silver. West Tibet, 10th-11th c. H. 26.7. John L. Severance Fund. 76.70

Caparisoned Elephant. Gilt bronze. China, Liao dynasty, 11th c. L. 24. Andrew R. and Martha Holden Jennings Fund. 80.24

Shokannon. Wood with poly-chromy and gold. Japan, Heian period, 10th c. H. 101.6. Leonard C. Hanna, Jr., Fund. 84.69

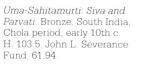

Salabhanjika: Female Divinity with a Tree. Sandstone. India, Rajasthan, from the Purana Mahadeva Temple (dated 973), Harsagiri. H. 54.6. Gift of Mr. and Mrs. Severance A. Millikin. 67.202

Nataraja: Siva as King of Dance. Bronze. South India, Chola period, 11th c. H. 111.5. Purchase from the J. H. Wade Fund. 30.331

Buddhist Retreat by Stream and Mountains. Hanging scroll, ink on silk. Attr. to Juran, Chinese, act. ca. 960-980, Northern Song dynasty. H. 185.4. Gift of Katharine Holden Thayer. 59.348

Jar. Glazed porcelain. China, Liao dynasty, 10th-11th c. H. 12.7. John L. Severance Fund. 57.29

Frieze of Musicians and Dancer. Sandstone. India, Rajasthan, from the Purana Mahadeva Temple (dated 973), Harsagiri. W. 95.3. John L. Severance Fund. 69.34

Ewer. Glazed stoneware with slip and underglaze painting. China, Liao dynasty, 11th c. H. 21.3. John L. Severance Fund. 53.248

32

Large Bowl. Earthenware. North America, New Mexico, Mimbres, ca. 1000-1200. D. 31.1. The Charles W. Harkness Endowment Fund. 30.50

Storage Jar. Earthenware. North America, Arizona, Anasazi culture, Tularosa black-on-white, ca. 1100-1250. H. 29.8. Purchase from the J. H. Wade Fund. 84.159

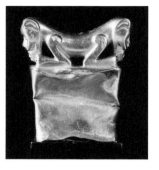

Double Puma Staff Head. Gold. Colombia, Quimbaya, ca. 1000. H. 8.2. Purchase from the J. H. Wade Fund. 44.319

Bird (Head of a Staff). Gold. Colombia, Quimbaya, ca. 1000. H. 7.5. John L. Severance Fund. 54.594

Seated Figure. Gold. Colombia, Quimbaya, ca. 1000. H. 7.3. The Norweb Collection. 39.509

Leaf from a Gradual and Sacramentary (Trier Ms. 151). Ink, tempera, and gold on parchment. Austria, Salzburg, early 11th c. H. 22.1. Purchase from the J. H. Wade Fund. 33.447

Tiraz. Tapestry weave; silk on linen. Egypt, Fatimid period, reign of al-Mustansir, 1049-50. H. 40.2. John L. Severance Fund. 50.528

Roundel. Tapestry weave; silk and gold on linen. Egypt, Fatimid period, late 11th c. H. 16.5. John L. Severance Fund. 50.541

Greek Gospels with Commentaries. Ink, tempera, and gold on parchment. Byzantium, 11th c. H. 29.4. Purchase from the J. H. Wade Fund. 42.152

St. Peter. Leaf from the *Epistles in a Manuscript (Pantokrator Ms. 49).* Ink, tempera, and gold on vellum. Byzantium, Constantinople, 11th c. H. 29.4. Purchase from the J. H. Wade Fund. 50.154

Seated Male Figure. Terracotta. Africa, Mali, Jenne area, ca. 1000-1300. H. 19.7. John L. Severance Fund. 85.199

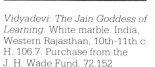

Goddess Uma. Gilt copper. Nepal, ca. 1000. H. 30.5. Leonard C. Hanna, Jr., Fund. 82.49

Kneeling Male Figure. Bronze. Cambodia, Baphuon style, 11th c.. H. 43.2. Leonard C. Hanna, Jr., Fund. 78.8

Siva. Gray sandstone. Cambodia, Baphuon style, 1st half 11th c. H. 76.5. Purchase from the J. H. Wade Fund. 41.25

Ewer: Cizhou Ware, Dengfeng Type. Glazed stoneware with slip. China, Northern Song dynasty, 10th-11th c. H. 17.5. Purchase from the J. H. Wade Fund. 48.219

Vidyadevi: The Jain Goddess of Learning. White marble. India, Western Rajasthan, 10th-11th c. H. 106.7. Purchase from the J. H. Wade Fund. 72.152

Shinto Deities. Wood (Japanese yew). Japan, Heian period, 10th-12th c. Max. H. 53.3. Leonard C. Hanna, Jr., Fund. 78.3-.4

Female Figure. Sandstone. Cambodia, late Baphuon style, 3d quarter 11th c. H. 91.4. Andrew R. and Martha Holden Jennings Fund. 70.60

Head of Siva. Tan sandstone. Cambodia, Angkor Wat style, 1st half 12th c. H. 41.9. Purchase from the J. H. Wade Fund. 40.53

Ewer: Yaozhou Ware Type. Glazed stoneware. China, Northern Song dynasty, late 10th-11th c. H. 18.3. Purchase from the J. H. Wade Fund. 48.220

Mithuna: Amorous Couple. Reddish sandstone. India, Madhya Pradesh, Khajuraho style, 11th c. H. 74. Leonard C. Hanna, Jr., Fund. 82.64

Avalokitesvara Padmapani Bodhisattva of Mercy Bearing a Lotus. Bronze. Nepal, ca. 11th c. H. 61.9. John L. Severance Fund. 76.3

Dancing Ganesha. Red sandstone. India, Khajuraho style, ca. 1000. H. 61.3. John L. Severance Fund. 61.93

England	Germany	Italy	Byzantium	Iran

34

Reliquary Casket. Boxwood. England, Anglo-Saxon, 2d half 10th c. H. 8.9. Purchase from the J. H. Wade Fund. 53.362

Portable Altar, Crosses of Countess Gertrude. From the Guelph Treasure. Gold, cloisonné enamel, semiprecious stones, and porphyry. Germany, Lower Saxony, Brunswick, ca. 1040. Altar: L. 26.7. Crosses: H. 24.2. Purchase from the J. H. Wade Fund with additional Gift from Mrs. E. B. Greene. 31.55 Gift of the John Huntington Art and Polytechnic Trust. 31.461-.462

Plaques from a Portable Altar. Ivory. Germany, Lower Rhine Valley, 2d half 11th c. H. each 5.1. Gift from J. H. Wade. 22.307-.309

Plaque: The Journey to Bethlehem. Ivory. South Italy, Campania, Amalfi workshop, ca. 1100-20. H. 16.4. Leonard C. Hanna, Jr., Fund. 78.40

"The Horn of St. Blasius." From the Guelph Treasure. Ivory. Sicily, 12th c. L. 48.9. Gift of the John Huntington Art and Polytechnic Trust. 30.740

St. Matthew. Leaf from a Gospel Book. Tempera and gold on vellum. Byzantium, Constantinople, 1057-63. H. 28.6. Purchase from the J. H. Wade Fund. 42.1512

Processional Cross (of St. Sabas). Gilt silver and niello. Byzantium, Constantinople, 11th c. W. 45.1 Leonard C. Hanna, Jr., Fund. 70.36

Pendant. Gilt silver, cloisonné enamel. Byzantium, probably Constantinople, 11th c. H. 5.1. Purchase from the J. H. Wade Fund. 72.94

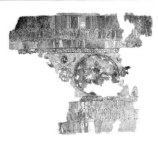

Fragment of a Large Cloth. Embroidery; silk on *mulham.* Iran or Iraq, Buyid period, 11th c. W. 40.5. Purchase from the J. H. Wade Fund. 38.300

Textile. Double cloth weave; silk. Iran or Iraq, Seljuk period, 11th c. H. 28. Gift of Ayyub Rabenou. 68.246

Siva's Trident with Ardha-narisvara: Half-Siva/Half-Parvati. Bronze. South India, Chola period, 11th-12th c. H. 35.5. Purchase from the J. H. Wade Fund. 69.117

Barbarian Royalty Worshipping Buddha. Handscroll, ink and color on silk. China, Northern Song dynasty, early 12th c. W. 103. Gift of Severance and Greta Millikin. 57.358

Vishnu Attended by Chakrapurusa and Shankhapurusa. Bronze with silver inlay. East India, Pala period, ca. 12th c. H. 43.5. Purchase from the J. H. Wade Fund. 64.453

Buddha Sheltered by Mucalinda, the Serpent King. Bronze. Cambodia, Angkor Wat style, early 12th c. H. 58.4. John L. Severance Fund. 63.263

Ganesha: Elephant-Headed God, Remover of Obstacles. Bronze. South India, Chola period, 12th c. H. 50.2. Gift of Katharine Holden Thayer. 70.62

Ladies of the Court (detail). Handscroll, ink and slight color on silk. China, Northern Song dynasty, early 12th c. Overall W. 168.5. John L. Severance Fund. 76.1

Brush Washer: Ru Ware. Glazed stoneware. China, Northern Song dynasty, early 12th c. D. 12.8. John L. Severance Fund. 57.40

Bodhisattva Manjusri: Lord of Wisdom. Image of gilded copper; pedestal and mandorla of brass. East India, Pala period, 11th-12th c. H. 31.2. Leonard C. Hanna, Jr., Fund. 60.285

Buddha Enthroned. Bronze. Cambodia, Angkor Wat style, 1st half 12th c. H. 26.7. Purchase from the J. H. Wade Fund. 42.149

Hanuman. Bronze. South India, Chola period, 12th c. H. 58.4. John L. Severance Fund. 80.26

Streams and Mountains Without End (detail). Handscroll, ink and slight color on silk. China, Northern Song dynasty, early 12th c. Overall W. 213. Gift of the Hanna Fund. 53.126

Top of an Incense Burner: Northern Celadon. Glazed stoneware. China, Northern Song dynasty, early 12th c. H. 18.4. Fanny Tewksbury King Collection. 66.26

Bird Pendant. Gold. Colombia, Tairona, 10th-mid 16th c. H. 6.3. In memory of Mr. and Mrs. Henry Humphreys, Gift of their daughter, Helen. 65.466

Capital: Fantastic Birds and Basilisk. Limestone. France, Bordelais (Dordogne), 12th c. H. 53.7. Purchase from the J. H. Wade Fund. 68.34

Portable Altar(?). Copper over wood core, champlevé enamel. Denmark, Schleswig, or North Germany, 12th c. H. 9.2. Purchase from the J. H. Wade Fund. 49.16

Plaque: Madonna and Child Enthroned with Angels. Ivory. Byzantium, 11th c. H. 25.4. Gift from J. H. Wade. 25.1293

Relief: Scenes from a Passion Cycle of Christ. Steatite. Byzantium, 11th-12th c. H. 11.8. Purchase from the J. H. Wade Fund. 62.27

Capital: Daniel Flanked by Lions. Limestone. France, possibly Poitou, 2d quarter 12th c. H. 34.3. John L. Severance Fund. 63.477

Casket. Copper over wood core with champlevé and cloisonné enamel. Germany, Lower Saxony, Hildesheim, ca. 1170-80. W. 21.3. Purchase from the J. H. Wade Fund. 49.431

Casket with Adam and Eve. Ivory over wood core. Byzantium, 11th-12th c. L. 46.7. Gift of J. H. Wade, John L. Severance, W. G. Mather, and F. F. Prentiss. 24.747

Capitals from Preuilly-sur-Claise. Limestone. France, Southern Touraine, mid 12th c. Max. H. 59. Gift of John L. Severance in memory of his wife, Elisabeth DeWitt Severance. 30.17

Plaque: Judgment and Martyrdom of St. Lawrence. Gilt copper and champlevé enamel. Germany, Lower Saxony, ca. 1180. H. 20.8. Purchase from the J. H. Wade Fund. 49.430

Textile: Basilisk Motive. Compound twill weave; silk. Byzantine, ca. 12th c. H. 34.5. Purchase from the J. H. Wade Fund. 74.99

Lion Incense Burner. Cast and engraved bronze. Iran, Seljuk period, 12th c. H. 36. John L. Severance Fund. 48.308

Textile. Tabby weave, block-printed, *mulham.* Iran, Seljuk period, 11th-12th c. W. 40. John L. Severance Fund. 50.558

Baluster Vase: Cizhou Ware. Lead-glazed stoneware with underglaze slip. China, Northern Song or Jin dynasty, 12th c. H. 32.1. Bequest of John L. Severance. 42.656

Meiping: Cizhou Ware. Glazed stoneware with slip and underglaze painting. China, Northern Song or Jin dynasty, 12th c. H. 35.9. Given in memory of James Campbell Weir. 86.245

Covered Box: Ding Ware. Glazed porcelain. China, Northern Song or Jin dynasty, 12th c. D. 10.5. John L. Severance Fund. 57.32

Cup and Stand: Qingbai Ware. Glazed porcelain. China, Southern Song dynasty, 12th c. Stand: D. 14. Gifts of Laurence H. Norton, Robert G. Norton, and Mrs. Miriam Norton White in memory of Mr. and Mrs. D. Z. Norton; Mrs. A. S. Chisholm; Horace E. Potter; and the John Huntington Art and Polytechnic Trust by exchange. 80.185,a

Bird-Shaped Vessel. Cast and engraved bronze, with turquoise eyes. Iran, Seljuk period, 12th-13th c. H. 17.5. Edward L. Whittemore Fund. 48.458

Pottery Jug. Underglaze slip-painted ware. Iran, Seljuk period, 12th c. H. 13.4. Edward L. Whittemore Fund. 47.495

Cloudy Mountains (detail). Handscroll, ink and slight color on silk, dated 1130. Mi Youren, Chinese, Southern Song dynasty. Overall W. 194.3. Purchase from the J. H. Wade Fund. 33.220

Pottery Bowl. Minai ware. Iran, early 13th c. D. 20.9. Gift of Leonard C. Hanna, Jr., for the Coralie Walker Hanna Memorial Collection. 39.214

Pottery Beaker. Minai ware. Iran, Rayy, late 12th-early 13th c. H. 13.5. Gift of the John Huntington Art and Polytechnic Trust. 17.977

Seated Arhat with Two Attendants. Hanging scroll, ink and color on silk. China, Southern Song dynasty, 1127-1279. H. 93.7. John L. Severance Fund. 76.91

Bodhisattva Samantabhadra. Hanging scroll, ink and color on silk. China, Southern Song dynasty, 1127-1279. H. 110.8. Mr. and Mrs. William H. Marlatt Fund. 62.161

Eleven-Headed Guanyin. Wood with traces of pigment and cut gold. China, Northern Song dynasty, early 12th c. H. 218.5. Purchase from the J. H. Wade Fund. 81.53

Guanyin. Wood with traces of gesso, pigment, and gilding. China, Southern Song dynasty, 12th c. H. 162.9. John L. Severance Fund. 80.80

38

Textile. Compound twill weave; silk. Spain, 12th c. W. 102.2. Purchase from the J. H. Wade Fund. 51.92

Miniature from a Bible: St. Luke. Ink, tempera, and gold on parchment. France, Burgundy, Cluny Abbey, ca. 1100. H. 17.1. Purchase from the J. H. Wade Fund. 68.190

Initial A from an Antiphonary: Tree of Jesse. Ink, tempera, gold, and silver on parchment. Meuse Valley, ca. 1115-25. H. 18.7. Mr. and Mrs. William H. Marlatt Fund. 49.202

Title Page of "Moralia of Gregorius" (now Engelberg). Ink and tempera on parchment. Attr. to Abbot Frowin, Switzerland, 1143-78. H. 27. Purchase from the J. H. Wade Fund. 55.74

Altar Cross. Gilt bronze. Germany, Lower Saxony, 3d quarter 12th c. H. 43.3. Purchase from the J. H. Wade Fund. 44.320

Textile. Lampas weave; silk. Spain, 12th c. W. 40.5. Purchase from the J. H. Wade Fund. 52.15

Reliquary. Gilt copper and champlevé enamel. Meuse Valley, ca. 1160. H. 19.7. Purchase from the J. H. Wade Fund. 26.428

Textile. Lampas weave; silk. Spain, 12th c. H. 43.2. Purchase from the J. H. Wade Fund. 50.146

Arm Reliquary. From Guelph Treasure. Gilt silver over oak core, champlevé enamel. Germany, Lower Saxony, Hildesheim, ca. 1180. H. 50.8. Gift of the John Huntington Art and Polytechnic Trust. 30.739

| Iran | Afghanistan | India | Java | China | Japan |

Bowl. Molded ceramic. Iran, probably Kashan, late Seljuk period, end 12th-beginning 13th c. D. 12.3. Leonard C. Hanna, Jr., Bequest. 85.20

Salver. Brass. Afghanistan, probably Herat or Ghazni, Ghaznavid period, 12th c. D. 58. John L. Severance Fund. 80.179

Bracket with Kala Mask. Volcanic stone. East Java, ca. 12th-14th c. H. 40. Norman O. Stone and Ella A. Stone Memorial Fund. 75.104

Bird on a Flowering Branch. Album leaf, ink and color on silk. China, Southern Song dynasty, 12th c. W. 24.5. The Kelvin Smith Collection, given by Mrs. Kelvin Smith. 85.371

Tabernacle. Lacquered wood with metal, glass, and color; cut gold leaf, and gold on interior. Japan, Heian period, 12th c. H. 160. John L. Severance Fund. 69.13

Dvarapala: Door Guardian of Siva. Stone. India, Mysore, Hoysala dynasty, 12th c. H. 113.4. John L. Severance Fund. 64.369

Pottery Jug. Luster ware. Iran, Rayy, Seljuk period, late 12th c. H. 35.5. Gift of the John Huntington Art and Polytechnic Trust. 15.525

Listening to the Qin. Fan painting, ink and slight color on silk. Liu Songnian, Chinese, act. 1170-1200, Southern Song dynasty. W. 24.6. Leonard C. Hanna, Jr., Fund. 83.85

Hanging Votive Image (Kakebotake). Gilt copper with engraving and repoussé. Japan, Heian period, 12th c. D. 52.5. Leonard C. Hanna, Jr., Fund. 85.16

Tombstone. Marble. Iran, Seljuk period, dated 1110. H. 64.5. Edward L. Whittemore Fund. 50.9

Processional Mask of a Bosatsu. Wood with lacquer and color. Japan, Heian period, late 12th c. H. 21.9. John L. Severance Fund. 50.581

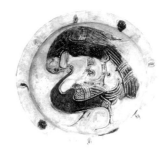

Corpus of Christ. Cast bronze with traces of gilding. Meuse Valley, 3d quarter 12th c. H. 9.9. Norman O. Stone and Ella A. Stone Memorial Fund. 69.50

Plaque: Hosea. Gilt copper, champlevé enamel, and niello. Germany, Lower Saxony, ca. 1180. H. 8.9. Purchase from the J. H. Wade Fund. 50.577

Capital: Angel (St. Matthew). Marble. North Italy, Bologna, last quarter 12th c. H. 33. Purchase from the J. H. Wade Fund. 72.21

Pottery Bowl. Lakabi ware. Iran, Kashan(?), Seljuk period, mid 12th c. D. 40.7. Purchase from the J. H. Wade Fund. 38.7

Columnar Figure of an Apostle. From Notre-Dame-en-Vaux, Châlons-sur-Marne. Limestone. France, ca. 1180. H. 97.8. General Income Fund. 19.38

Corpus of Christ. Polychromed wood. France, 3d quarter 12th c. H. 110.5. Leonard C. Hanna, Jr., Fund. 80.1

Cross. Gilt copper and champlevé enamel. Master of the Royal Plantagenet workshop, French, Limoges, ca. 1190. H. 67. Gift from J. H. Wade. 23.1051

Nativity. From a Gospel Book (now *Trier*). Tempera, silver, and gold on parchment. Lower Saxony, Helmarshausen, end 12th c. H. 34.4. Purchase from the J. H. Wade Fund. 33.445

Griffin (one of a pair). Marble. North Italy, ca. 1220. L. 120.7. Gift of the John Huntington Art and Polytechnic Trust. 28.861

Pottery Bowl. Champlevé ware. Iran, Garruz District, Seljuk period, 12th c. D. 39.2. Purchase from the J. H. Wade Fund. 38.8

Pottery Plate. Luster ware. Iran, Rayy, Seljuk period, late 12th-early 13th c. D. 39.4. John L. Severance Fund. 51.289

Gandavyuha: Structure of the World (detail). Ink and color on palm leaf. East India, Pala period, 11th-12th c. Overall W. 52.4. Purchase from the J. H. Wade Fund. 55.49

Astasahasrika Prajnaparamita: Book of Transcendental Wisdom (detail). Color on palm leaf. Nepal, 1100. Overall W. 56.2. Purchase from the J. H. Wade Fund. 38.301

Sunflower Bowl: Guan Ware. Glazed porcelain. China, Southern Song dynasty, 1127-1279. D. 17.5. Gift of Severance and Greta Millikin. 57.66

Basin with Inlaid Figures and Calligraphy. Bronze inlaid with silver. Korea, Koryo period, 12th c. W. 28.3. Leonard C. Hanna, Jr., Fund. 85.112

Incense Burner: Guan Ware. Glazed porcelain. China, Southern Song dynasty, 1127-1279. W. 15.5. Gift of Mr. and Mrs. Severance A. Millikin. 57.63

Prunus Vase (Maebyong). Iron-glazed porcelaneous ware with underglaze design. Korea, Koryo period, 12th c. H. 29. Purchase from the J. H. Wade Fund. 61.270

Basin: Guan Ware. Glazed porcelain with copper rim. China, Southern Song dynasty, 1127-1279. D. 24.2. John L. Severance Fund. 57.48

Plaque from a Châsse: The Crucifixion and the Martyrdom of St. Thomas Becket. Gilt copper and champlevé enamel, ca. 1220-25. Attr. to Master G. Alpais and workshop, French, Limoges. W. 28.4. Purchase from the J. H. Wade Fund. 51.449

Mourning Virgin. From a Crucifixion group. Gilt bronze. Meuse Valley, early 13th c. H. 10.2. Gift of Mrs. Chester D. Tripp. 70.35

Monstrance with the Paten of St. Bernward. From the Guelph Treasure. Paten: gilt silver and niello, 3d quarter 12th c. Master of the Oswald Reliquary. Monstrance: gilt silver and rock crystal. Germany, Lower Saxony, Hildesheim, end 14th c. H. 34.4. Purchase from the J. H. Wade Fund with additional Gift from Mrs. R. Henry Norweb. 30.50

Reliquary in the Form of a Book. From Guelph Treasure. Ivory: Meuse Valley, Liège, ca. 1000. Frame: Lower Saxony, Brunswick, ca. 1340. H. 31.8. Gift of the John Huntington Art and Polytechnic Trust. 30.741

Frieze with Apsaras. Sandstone. Cambodia, Bayon style, late 12th-early 13th c. H. 87.7. Purchase from the J. H. Wade Fund. 38.433

Relief of an Apsara. Sandstone. Cambodia, Angkor Thom, possibly from the Terrace of the Leper King, late 12th-early 13th c. H. 61. Purchase from the J. H. Wade Fund. 38.304

Head of Lokesvara. Sandstone. Cambodia, Bayon style, late 12th-early 13th c. H. 35.3. Purchase from the J. H. Wade Fund. 55.47

Finial with the Temptation of Buddha by Mara. Bronze. Cambodia, Bayon style, late 12th-early 13th c. H. 39.2. Andrew R. and Martha Holden Jennings Fund. 64.93

Bamboo in Winter. One of pair of hanging scrolls, ink on silk. China, Southern Song dynasty, 1127-1279. H. 133.7. Leonard C. Hanna, Jr., Fund. 82.151

Woodcutters Returning Home. Hanging scroll, ink on silk. China, Southern Song dynasty, 1127-1279. H. 124.5. Leonard C. Hanna, Jr., Fund. 88.20

Vase in the Shape of a Bamboo Shoot. Celadon porcelain with incised design. Korea, Koryo period, 12th c. H. 25.4. Elisabeth Severance Prentiss Collection. 44.164

Iconographical Sketch for a Mandala (detail). Hanging scroll, ink on paper. Japan, Heian period, 12th c. Overall H. 122.1. Leonard C. Hanna, Jr., Fund. 87.39

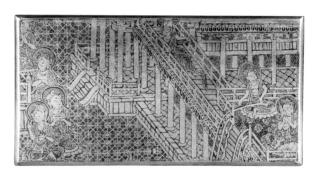

Alms Bowl with Landscape Design. Bronze with incised decoration. Korea, Koryo period, 12th-13th c. D. 27. Leonard C. Hanna, Jr., Fund. 86.94

Western Paradise Scene. Lacquer on wood, fragment mounted as a box cover. Japan, Heian period, ca. 1200. W. 13.2. John L. Severance Fund. 61.91

Willow and Magpie. Hanging scroll, ink on paper. Attr. to Mu Qi, Chinese, 1177-1239, Southern Song dynasty, H. 60.4. John L. Severance Fund. 82.53

Dragon. Hanging scroll, ink on silk (one of pair). Attr. to Mu Qi, Chinese, 1177-1239, Southern Song dynasty. H. 123.9. Purchase from the J. H. Wade Fund. 58.428

1000-1399

England	Spain	Germany	Syria	Iraq	Iran

44

Christ in Majesty. From a Psalter. Ink, tempera, and gold on parchment. England, Abbey of Peterborough(?), ca. 1235. L. 19. Mr. and Mrs. William H. Marlatt Fund. 45.132

Textile. Compound weave; silk and gold. Spain, 13th c. H. 16.5. Purchase from the J. H. Wade Fund. 32.137

Lion Aquamanile. Brass. Germany, Lower Saxony, probably Hildesheim, mid 13th c. H. 26.2. Gift of Mrs. Chester D. Tripp in honor of Chester D. Tripp. 72.167

Box. Bronze, inlaid with gold and silver. Syria, 13th c. H. 9.9. Purchase from the J. H. Wade Fund. 44.482

Three Physicians Preparing Medicine. From Dioscorides's *Materia Medica* in Arabic. Opaque watercolor on paper, dated 1224. 'Abd Allah ibn al-Fadl, Iraqi. H. 33.3. John L. Severance Fund. 77.91

Ewer. Brass, inlaid with silver, dated 1223. Ahmad al-Dhaki, al-Naqsh, al-Mawsili, Iraq, Mosul. H. 38.1. John L. Severance Fund. 56.11

Textile. Lampas weave; silk. Spain, ca. 1279. H. 9.9. Purchase from the J. H. Wade Fund. 42.1077

Processional Cross. Gilt copper and champlevé enamel over wood core. Germany, Upper Rhine, Lake Constance, end 13th c. H. 50.2. Purchase from the J. H. Wade Fund. 42.1091

Candlestick. Engraved brass, inlaid with silver. Syria, 2d half 13th c. H. 24.8. Purchase from the J. H. Wade Fund. 51.539

Textile. Tabby weave with supplementary weft; silk. Iran or Syria, 1st half 13th c. H. 22.8. Purchase from the J. H. Wade Fund. 39.506

Textile. Tapestry weave; silk and gold. Spain, Hispano-Islamic period, 13th c. H. 17.4. Purchase from the J. H. Wade Fund. 52.105

Tray. Brass, inlaid with silver. Syria, mid 13th c. D. 54. Purchase from the J. H. Wade Fund and part donation from H. Kevorkian. 45.386

Pottery Wall Tile. Luster ware. Iran, Kashan, Il-Khanid period, 1266. H. 20. Gift of the John Huntington Art and Polytechnic Trust. 15.524

Footed Bowl. Bronze, inlaid with silver. Iran, Seljuk period, early 13th c. H. 11.5. Purchase from the J. H. Wade Fund. 44.485

Gibbon. Fan painting, ink and slight color on silk. Attr. to Xia Gui, Chinese, act. 1180-1224, Southern Song dynasty. W. 26.5. John L. Severance Fund. 78.1

Dish: Longqhuan Ware. Glazed porcelain. China, Southern Song dynasty, 13th c. D. 21.3. Severance and Greta Millikin Collection. 64.164

Arhat. Hanging scroll, ink and light color on silk. Korea, Koryo period, ca. 1235. H. 52.5. Purchase from the J. H. Wade Fund. 79.71

Saiva Saint, Manikkavachakar. Bronze. South India, 12th-13th c. H. 33.5. John L. Severance Fund. 67.148

Vajrasattva Buddha and Acolytes. Color and gold on canvas. Central Tibet, 2d half 12th c. H. 111. Mr. and Mrs. William H. Marlatt Fund. 89.104

Cloth of Gold. Lampas weave; silk and gold thread. Sino-Islamic, after 1220. H. 124.5. Purchase from the J. H. Wade Fund. 89.50

Incense Burner: Longqhuan Ware. Glazed porcelain. China, Southern Song dynasty, 13th c. D. 13.9. John L. Severance Fund. 54.790

Meiping: Jizhou Ware. Stoneware with slip painting. China, Southern Song dynasty, 13th c. H. 26.3. Gifts of J. H. Wade and Mr. and Mrs. J. H. Wade; and Purchase from the J. H. Wade Fund by exchange. 80.186

Two Lamas Discussing the Dharma. Color on cloth. Tibet, late 12th-early 13th c. H. 51.4. John L. Severance Fund. 87.146

Sakyamuni and Two Attendants. Hanging scroll, ink, color, and gold on silk. Korea, Koryo period, ca. 1300. H. 217.8. John L. Severance Fund. 82.25

Narasimha: Lion Incarnation of Vishnu. Bronze. South India, Chola period, ca. 13th c. H. 55.2. Gift of Dr. Norman Zaworski. 73.187

Head of an Apostle. Limestone. Northeast France, Thérouanne, ca. 1235. H. 44.6. Leonard C. Hanna, Jr., Fund. 78.56

Pair of Angels. Walnut with traces of paint and gilding. Northeast France, probably Reims, ca. 1235-45. Max. H. 78.7. Leonard C. Hanna, Jr., Fund. 66.360, 67.27

Relief Appliqué: Enthroned Madonna and Child. Gilt copper and enameled pearls. France, Limoges, 2d quarter 13th c. H. 21.6. Purchase from the J. H. Wade Fund. 62.29

Mourning Virgin and St. John from a Crucifixion Group. Painted wood. Austria, Salzburg, mid 13th c. H. 43.8. Gift of Severance and Greta Millikin. 57.500, 58.189

Reliquary of the True Cross. Silver gilt and niello, dated 1214. South Italy. H. 43. Purchase from the J. H. Wade Fund. 52.89

Madonna and Child with Saints. Tempera on panel, 1230s. Berlinghiero, Italian, Lucca. W. 51.5. Gift of the John Huntington Art and Polytechnic Trust. 66.237

The Deposition. From a Psalter (now Warsaw Nat. Lib. Ms. 8003). Ink, tempera, and gold on vellum. Master of the Potocki workshop, French, Paris, ca. 1240-50. L. 15.4. Mr. and Mrs. William H. Marlatt Fund. 85.80

The Virgin and St. John from a Crucifixion Group. Painted and gilded wood. Spain, Castile, ca. 1275. H. 141.1 and 154.9. Gift of Mr. and Mrs. Francis F. Prentiss. 30.621-.622

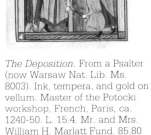

Quadrilobed Plaque. Gold with cloisonné and translucent enamel, ca. 1300. Circle of Guillaume Julien, French, Paris. H. 4.8. The Mary Spedding Milliken Memorial Collection.* 32.537

Stained Glass Panel with Aconite Leaves. Pot metal and grisaille. France, Alsace, ca. 1275. H. 55.9. Gift of Mrs. Elsa Brummer. 77.89

A Pope and Assistants Celebrating Mass: Initial G. From a Choral Book. Tempera on parchment. Italy, Bologna(?), ca. 1300. L. 22.9. Gift from J. H. Wade. 24.101

Hitching Post. Limestone. Iran, Hamadan(?), Il-Khanid period, 13th c. H. 61.9. Purchase from the J. H. Wade Fund. 44.481

Panel. Lampas weave; silk with flat and wrapped gold thread. Western Central Asia, prob. mid 13th c. H. 170.5. Purchase from the J. H. Wade Fund. 90.2

Sakyamuni Descending from the Mountains. Hanging scroll, ink on paper, dated 1244. China, Southern Song dynasty. H. 74.6. John L. Severance Fund. 70.2

White-Robed Guanyin. Hanging scroll, ink on paper. Attrib. to Zhang Yuehu, Chinese, late 13th c., Yuan dynasty. H. 104. Leonard C. Hanna, Jr., Fund. 72.160

White-Robed Kannon. From Kozan-ji, Kyoto. Hanging scroll, ink on paper. Japan, Kamakura period, ca. 1200. H. 91.5. John L. Severance Fund. 51.540

Amida, Buddha of the Western Paradise. Wood, cut gold leaf and polychromy, dated 1269. Koshun and assistants, Japanese, Kamakura period. H. 94.6. John L. Severance Fund. 60.197

End of Balustrade. Limestone, dated 1304. Iran, Hamadan(?), Il-Khanid period. H. 66.7. Purchase from the J. H. Wade Fund. 38.15

Fragment from a Cope. Lampas weave; silk, cotton, and silver thread. U.S.S.R., Central Asia (Transoxiana), late 13th-early 14th c. H. 42.5. Purchase from the J. H. Wade Fund. 85.4

Scholar Reclining and Watching Rising Clouds. Fan painting mounted as album leaf, ink and slight color on silk. Ma Lin, act. mid 13th c. Southern Song dynasty. H. 25.3. John L. Severance Fund. 61.421

Poem by Wang Wei (699-759). Fan calligraphy mounted as album leaf, ink on silk, orig. mounted with *Scholar Reclining and Watching Rising Clouds,* dated 1256. Emperor Lizong, Southern Song dynasty. H. 25.1. John L. Severance Fund. 61.422

Red Amida. Hanging scroll, ink, color, and cut gold leaf on silk. Japan, Kamakura period, 1185-1333. H. 127. Leonard C. Hanna, Jr., Fund. 71.164

Zao Gongen. Wood with lacquer. Japan, Heian-Kamakura period, 13th c. H. 106.7. Purchase from the J. H. Wade Fund. 73.105

Nushirwan's Fifth Banquet for Buzurdjmir. From *Shahnama of Firdawsi.* Opaque watercolor on paper. Iran, Tabriz, Il-Khanid period, ca. 1330-40. H. 24.2. John L. Severance Fund. 59.330

Portrait of Fujiwara Kamatari. Hanging scroll, ink, color, and cut gold leaf on silk. Japan, Kamakura period, 1185-1333. H. 141.3. Leonard C. Hanna, Jr., Fund. 83.5

Spain	France	Germany	Egypt	Syria

Albarello. Maiolica. Spain, Valencia, Paterna, 14th c. H. 21.6. In memory of Mr. and Mrs. Henry Humphreys, Gift of their daughter, Helen. 45.28

The War in Heaven. From an *Apocalypse.* Ink, tempera, and gold on parchment. France, Lorraine, ca. 1295. W. 14.2. John L. Severance Fund. 83.74

Initial I: Scenes from the Life of St. Augustine. Ink, tempera, gold on parchment. Second Master of Wettinger Gradual, Cologne(?), 14th c. H. 57.8.William H. Marlatt Fund.* 49.203

Textile. Tabby weave, block-printed; cotton. Egypt, Mamluk period, 13th-14th c. H. 17.2. Purchase from the J. H. Wade Fund. 29.845

Device for Washing Hands. From *Automata* by Al-Jazari. Opaque watercolor and gold on paper. Syria, Damascus(?), Mamluk period, 1315. H. 31.3. Purchase from the J. H. Wade Fund and part donation from H. Kevorkian. 45.383

Textile. Lampas weave; silk. Spain, Granada, 14th c. H. 49. Purchase from the J. H. Wade Fund. 39.35

Textile. Lampas weave; silk. Spain, Granada, 14th c. H. 76.8. Purchase from the J. H. Wade Fund. 46.417

Virgin and Child. Limestone with traces of paint and gilding. France, Lorraine, ca. 1310-20. H. 75.8. Leonard C. Hanna, Jr., Fund. 74.14

Christ and John the Evangelist. Painted wood. Germany, Swabia, early 14th c. H. 92.7. Purchase from the J. H. Wade Fund. 28.753

Mosque Lamp. Enameled and gilded glass. Syria, Damascus (or Egypt, Cairo?), Mamluk period, ca. 1315. H. 39.5. John L. Severance Fund. 81.10

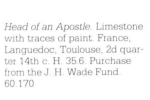

Head of an Apostle. Limestone with traces of paint. France, Languedoc, Toulouse, 2d quarter 14th c. H. 35.6. Purchase from the J. H. Wade Fund. 60.170

Diptych: Consecration of St. Martin of Tours and St. Martin Dividing His Cloak with a Beggar. Ivory. Germany, Rhenish, 2d quarter 14th c. H. 9. Purchase from the J. H. Wade Fund. 71.103

Bowl. Enameled glass. Egypt or Syria, Mamluk period, 14th c. D. 31.8. Purchase from the J. H. Wade Fund. 44.235

Bowl. White jade (nephrite). China, Yuan dynasty, late 13th-early 14th c. W. 15.9. Anonymous Gift. 52.510

Spouted Bowl: Longquan Ware. Glazed stoneware with copper red spots. China, Yuan dynasty, early 14th c. D. 17.5. Leonard C. Hanna, Jr., Fund. 85.109

Bahram Gur Slays a Dragon. From *Shahnama of Firdawsi.* Opaque watercolor and gold on paper. Iran, Tabriz school(?), Il-Khanid period, ca. 1330-40. H. 19.7. Grace Rainey Rogers Fund. 43.658

Tanka with Green Tara. Color on cloth. Tibet, ca. 13th c. H. 52.1. Purchase from the J. H. Wade Fund by exchange. 70.156

The Poet Taira no Kanemori. Section of a handscroll mounted as a hanging scroll, ink and color on paper. Japan, Kamakura period, 1185-1333. W. 46.7. John L. Severance Fund. 51.397

River Village: Fishermen's Joy. Fan painting mounted as album leaf, ink and color on silk. Zhao Mengfu, Chinese, 1254-1322, Yuan dynasty. W. 30. Leonard C. Hanna, Jr., Fund. 78.66

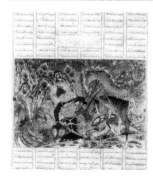

Textile. Lampas weave; silk and gold thread. Iran or Iraq, 14th c. W. 33.7. Purchase from the J. H. Wade Fund. 39.44

Enno Gyoja. Lacquered wood. Japan, Kamakura period, 1185-1333. H. 74.9. Purchase from the J. H. Wade Fund. 75.65

One of the "Ten Fast Bulls." Section of a handscroll mounted as a hanging scroll, ink and light color on paper. Japan, Kamakura period, ca. 1300. W. 32.1. John L. Severance Fund. 52.286

Bamboo, Rocks, and Lonely Orchids. Handscroll, ink on paper. Zhao Mengfu, Chinese, 1254-1322, Yuan dynasty. W. 144.2. John L. Severance Fund. 63.515

Box with Chrysanthemum Design. Lacquer on wood. Japan, Kamakura period, 1185-1333. W. 27.3. John L. Severance Fund. 63.513

Suibyo (Ewer) for Holy Water. Bronze. Japan, Kamakura period, 1185-1333. H. 27. Bequest of Elizabeth M. Skala. 90.17

Angel from an Annunciation Group (Virgin: Paris, Musée du Louvre). Marble, paint, and gold. France, mid 14th c. H. 56.5. Purchase from the J. H. Wade Fund. 54.387

Virgin and Child. Painted lindenwood. Upper Austria, ca. 1370-80. H. 54. John L. Severance Fund. 62.207

Frontispiece of the Mariegola of the Scuola di San Giovanni Evangelista. Tempera and gold on parchment. Venice, 1st third 14th c. L. 27.3. Delia E. and L. E. Holden Funds. 59.128

Cofanetto. Painted and gilded wood. Italy, Siena, 14th c. L. 41.3. John L. Severance Fund. 54.600

Old Trees by a Cool Spring. Hanging scroll, ink on silk, dated 1326. Li Shixing, Chinese, Yuan dynasty. H. 165.7. Purchase from the J. H. Wade Fund. 70.4

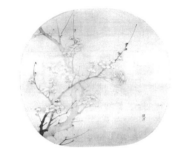

The Annunciation. Oil on panel, late 14th c. French Master. H. 35.2. Mr. and Mrs. William H. Marlatt Fund. 54.393

Virgin and Child from Maria-pfarr im Lungau. Stone. Austria, ca. 1395. H. 101.9. Purchase from the J. H. Wade Fund. 65.236

Madonna and Child. Marble, ca. 1330s. Attr. to Andrea Pisano, Italian. H. 37.6. Leonard C. Hanna, Jr., Fund. 72.51

Polyptych: Virgin and Child with St. Francis, John the Baptist, St. James the Great, and Mary Magdalen. Tempera on panel, ca. 1315-20. Ugolino da Siena, Italian, Siena.

W. 192.5. Leonard C. Hanna, Jr. Fund. 61.40

Plum Blossoms in Moonlight. Fan painting mounted as album leaf, ink on silk. Yan Hui, Chinese, act. early 14th c., Yuan dynasty. W. 27.6. Andrew R. and Martha Holden Jennings Fund. 78.49

Coin: Mouton d'Or, Jean le Bon. Gold. France, 1350-64. D. 3. The Norweb Collection. 64.372

Miniature: Two Female Saints. Tempera and gold on parchment. Niccolo di ser Sozzo Tegliacci, Italian, Siena, act. 1334-36. L. 8.3. Gift from J. H. Wade. 24.430

Pair of Angels. Marble, ca. 1350. Attr. to Giovanni and Pacio da Firenze, Italian. Max. H. 99.7. Gift of the John Huntington Art and Polytechnic Trust. 25.1343-.1344

Sakyamuni as an Ascetic. Gilt bronze. China, Yuan dynasty, early 14th c. H. 44.2. Purchase from the J. H. Wade Fund. 66.116

Three Horses and Four Grooms (detail). Handscroll, ink and color on silk. Ren Renfa, Chinese, 1254-1327, Yuan dynasty. Overall W. 136.8. Leonard C. Hanna, Jr., Fund. 60.181

Miroku, The Future Buddha. Wood with lacquer, polychromy, and cut gold leaf. Japan, Kamakura period, 13th c. H. 64.8. Leonard C. Hanna, Jr., Fund. 83.18

Portrait of Hoto Kokushi (Priest Kakushin). Wood with lacquer. From Myoshin-ji, Wakayama Prefecture, Kamakura period, ca. 1286. H. 91.4. Leonard C. Hanna, Jr., Fund. 70.67

Jar with Scenes of Frolicking Monkeys. Negoro lacquer on wood, dated 1302. Japan, Kamakura period. H. 49.4. Leonard C. Hanna, Jr., Fund. 84.8

Shotoku Taishi. Wood with lacquer and traces of color. Japan, Kamakura period, early 14th c. H. 68.6. Gift in memory of Dr. and Mrs. William Hawksley Weir. 89.76

The Lantern Night Excursion of Zhong Kui (detail). Handscroll, ink and slight color on silk. Yan Hui, Chinese, act. early 14th c., Yuan dynasty. Overall W. 240.3. Mr. and Mrs. William H. Marlatt Fund. 61.206

Taima Mandala (detail). Hanging scroll, ink, color, gold, and silver pigment, and *kirikane* (cut gold leaf) on silk. Japan, Kamakura period, ca. 1300. Overall H. 140. The Severance and Greta Millikin Purchase Fund. 90.82

Monju and Attendants. Hanging scroll, ink and color on silk. Japan, Kamakura period, 13th c. H. 96. Mr. and Mrs. William H. Marlatt Fund. 86.1

Kumano Mandala: The Three Sacred Shrines. Hanging scroll, ink and color on silk. Japan, Kamakura period, ca. 1300. H. 134. John L. Severance Fund. 53.16

Nika Byakudo: The White Path to the Western Paradise Across Two Rivers. Hanging scroll, ink and color on silk. Japan, Kamakura period, 13th-14th c. H. 123.5. Gift of the Norweb Foundation. 55.44

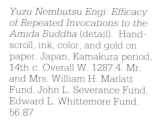

Table Screen with Depiction of Peach Blossom Spring. Lacquered wood with mother-of-pearl inlay. Yuan dynasty, 14th c. H. 48.9. The Severance and Greta Millikin Purchase Fund. 78.2

Raft-Cup. Cast silver with engraving, dated 1345. Zhu Bishan, Chinese, Yuan dynasty. L. 20.5. John L. Severance Fund. 77.7

Yuzu Nembutsu Engi: Efficacy of Repeated Invocations to the Amida Buddha (detail). Handscroll, ink, color, and gold on paper. Japan, Kamakura period, 14th c. Overall W. 1287.4. Mr. and Mrs. William H. Marlatt Fund, John L. Severance Fund, Edward L. Whittemore Fund. 56.87

Altar Cloth. Embroidery; linen on linen. Germany, Altenberg an der Lahn, 2d quarter 14th c. W. 381. Purchase from the J. H. Wade Fund. 48.352

Uma-Mahesvara: Parvati-Siva. Gilt copper. Nepal, ca. 14th c. H. 29.8. Leonard C. Hanna, Jr., Fund. 84.3

The Gotha Missal (Use of Paris), Fols. 63v-64r: The Crucifixion and Christ in Majesty. Ink, tempera, and gold on parchment, ca. 1360-65. Jean Bondol and workshop, French, Paris. H. 27.2. Mr. and Mrs. William H. Marlatt Fund. 62.287

Lily and Butterflies. Hanging scroll, ink on silk. Liu Shanshou, Chinese, act. 14th c., Yuan dynasty. H. 160. Purchase from the J. H. Wade Fund. 71.132

Enthroned Virgin and Child. Ivory. Germany (?), 14th c. H. 13.3. Gift of Mrs. Edward B. Greene. 28.760

Crucified Christ. Walnut. Germany, Cologne, 1380-90. H. 41.5. Andrew R. and Martha Holden Jennings Fund. 81.52

The Calvary with a Carthusian Monk. Tempera on panel, ca. 1390-95. Jean de Beaumetz, French, Burgundy, and workshop. H. 56.5. Leonard C. Hanna, Jr., Fund. 64.454

Virgin and Child. Painted limestone. France, Central Loire Valley, ca. 1385-90. H. 54.6. Purchase from the J. H. Wade Fund. 62.28

Diptych: Four Scenes from the Life of Christ. Ivory. Germany(?), 3d quarter 14th c. H. 20.6. Andrew R. and Martha Holden Jennings Fund. 84.158a

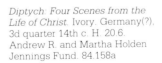

Plum Blossoms in Moonlight. Hanging scroll, ink on silk. Wang Mian, Chinese, 1287-1366, Yuan dynasty. H. 164.5. Leonard C. Hanna, Jr., Fund. 74.26

Poetic Feeling in a Thatched Pavilion (detail). Handscroll, ink on paper, dated 1347. Wu Zhen, Chinese, Yuan dynasty. Overall W. 99.4. Leonard C. Hanna, Jr., Fund. 63.259

Dish with Dragons: Longquan Ware. Glazed stoneware with molded biscuit decoration. China, Yuan dynasty, 14th c. D. 16.5. Severance and Greta Millikin Collection. 64.183

Fluted Cup with Dragon Handle: Qingbai Ware. Glazed porcelain. China, Yuan dynasty, early 14th c. D. 9. Severance and Greta Millikin Collection. 64.163

Avalokitesvara. Hanging scroll, ink and color on silk with inscription in gold ink on silk. Korea, Koryo period, 14th c. H. 155. The Severance and Greta Millikin Purchase Fund. 86.8

Bato Kannon. Wood with slight color. Japan, from Hodarakuson-ji, Wakayama Prefecture, Kamakura period, 1185-1333. H. 82.6. John L. Severance Fund. 81.1

Leisure Enough to Spare. Handscroll, ink on paper, dated 1360. Yao Tingmei, Chinese, Yuan dynasty. W. 84. John L. Severance Fund. 54.791

Jar. Porcelain with underglaze blue decoration. China, Yuan dynasty, 14th c. H. 39.3. John L. Severance Fund. 62.154

Tahoto (Reliquary). Wood with lacquer, metal, color, and gold on painted images. Kamakura-Nambokucho period, 14th c. H. 35.2. John L. Severance Fund. 82.8

The Nine Songs (detail). Handscroll, ink on paper. Zhang Wu, Chinese, 1335-65, Yuan dynasty. Overall W. 438.2. Purchase from the J. H. Wade Fund. 59.138

Bodhidharma Crossing the Yangzi River on a Reed. Hanging scroll, ink on paper. China, Yuan dynasty, 1279-1368. H. 89.2. John L. Severance Fund. 64.44

Second Coming of the Fifth Patriarch. Handscroll section mounted as hanging scroll, ink on paper. Yintuoluo, ca. mid 14th c., Yuan dynasty. W. 45.5. Purchase from the J. H. Wade Fund. 67.211

Mexico   England   France   Italy

54

Maize-Carrying Deity. Stone.
Mexico, Aztec, 1350-1519.
H. 27.6. The Norweb Collection.
49.555

Stone Monkey. Mexico,
Tacubaya, Aztec, 1350-1519.
H. 24.5. Gift of William Ellery
Greene. 59.125

*Seated Figure of Tlaloc, The
Rain God.* Serpentine. Mexico,
Aztec. 1350-1519. H. 28.6.
Purchase from the J. H. Wade
Fund. 66.361

Orphrey: Tree of Jesse.
Embroidery (opus Anglicanum);
silk, gold, and silver threads on
linen. England, mid 14th c.
H. 99. Purchase from the J. H.
Wade Fund. 49.503

*Diptych: Scenes from the Flag-
ellation, Crucifixion, Resurrec-
tion and Noli me Tangere.* Ivory.
France, Ile-de-France, 14th c.
H. 16.8. Gift of Mrs. Chester D.
Tripp in memory of Chester D.
Tripp. 75.110

Initial L with St. Lucy. From an
Antiphonary. Ink, tempera, and
gold on parchment. Master of
Dominican Effigies, Italian, ca.
1335-45. H. 44.3. Purchase from
the J. H. Wade Fund. 52.281

Textile. Lampas weave; silk and
gold thread. Italy, last 3d 14th c.
H. 24.5. Purchase from the J. H.
Wade Fund. 43.283

Textile. Velvet weave; silk. Italy,
last quarter 14th c. W. 26.7.
Purchase from the J. H. Wade
Fund. 39.43

*Fragment of a Chasuble with
Orphrey* (detail). Lampas
weave; silk and gold. Italy, last
3d 14th c. *Orphrey:* Compound
twill weave; silk, linen, and gold.
Germany, Cologne, late 14th c.
Overall H. 106.8. Purchase from
the J. H. Wade Fund. 28.653

*Miniature from a Missal: The
Crucifixion.* Tempera and gold
on parchment, signed: *Nicolaus
F.* Niccolò da Bologna, Italian,
act. ca. 1369-1402. H. 26. Gift
from J. H. Wade. 24.1013

Goddess Vajravarahi. Gilt bronze. Tibet, 14th-15th c. H. 36. Leonard C. Hanna, Jr., Fund. 82.50

Textile. Lampas weave with compound tabby weave; silk and gold thread. China, Yuan dynasty, 1260-1368. H. 43.7. Purchase from the J. H. Wade Fund. 48.204

Bamboo, Rock, and Tall Tree. Hanging scroll, ink on paper. Ni Zan, Chinese, 1301-74, Yuan dynasty. H. 67.3. Leonard C. Hanna, Jr., Fund. 78.65

Fukutomi Zoshi (detail). Handscroll, ink and color on paper. Japan, Kamakura period, 14th c. Overall W. 1038.8. John L. Severance Fund. 53.358

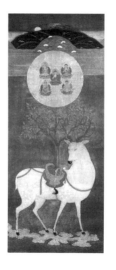

Raigo: Descent of Amida. Hanging scroll, ink, color, and gold on silk. Japan, Kamakura period, 14th c. H. 170.2. John L. Severance Fund. 53.123

Ink Flowers (detail). Handscroll, ink on paper, dated 1361. Zhao Zhong, Chinese, Yuan dynasty. Overall W. 153.2. John L. Severance Fund. 67.36

Yujo Monogatari Emaki. Section of a handscroll mounted as a hanging scroll, ink on paper. Japan, Nambokucho-Muromachi period, 14th-15th c. W. 33. John L. Severance Fund. 85.132

Rock, Bamboo, and Orchids. Hanging scroll, ink on paper. Bompo, Japanese, 1348-ca. 1420, Muromachi period. H. 79.2. John L. Severance Fund. 72.15

Plate: Jun Ware. Glazed stoneware. China, Yuan dynasty, 1279-1368. D. 18.1. Bequest of John L. Severance. 42.665

Fluted Bowl: Jun Ware. Glazed stoneware. China, Yuan dynasty, 1279-1368. D. 23.5. John L. Severance Fund. 57.33

Aizen Myoo (Lord of Human Desire). Wood with lacquer and color. Japan, Nambokucho period, 14th c. H. 75. Bequest of Elizabeth M. Skala. 87.185

Kasuga Mandala. Hanging scroll, ink, color, and gold on silk. Japan, Nambokucho-Muromachi period, 14th-15th c. H. 95.5. Leonard C. Hanna, Jr., Fund. 88.19

Pectoral Ornament. Gold and jade. Mexico, Mixtec or Aztec, 1350-1519. H. 8. Gift of James C. Gruener in memory of his wife, Florence Crowell Gruener. 83.190

Table Fountain. Silver gilt and translucent enamel. France, Avignon, 1st half 14th c. H. 31.1. Gift from J. H. Wade. 24.859

Medallion from a Chain. Gold, enamel, and pearls. Franco-Flemish, ca. 1400. D. 4.4. Purchase from the J. H. Wade Fund. 47.507

Enthroned Madonna with Christ Child. Limestone with polychromy and gilding. Franco-Flemish, ca. 1400. H. 44.8. John L. Severance Fund. 70.13

Three Mourners from the Tomb of Philip the Bold (Chartreuse de Champmol). Alabaster, 1404-1406. Claus Sluter and Claus de Werve, Franco-Flemish (act. Burgundy). Max. H. 41.9.

Purchase from the J. H. Wade Fund. 40.128; Bequest of Leonard C. Hanna, Jr. 58.66-.67

Figure of a Warrior. Gold. Mexico, Aztec, 1400-1519. H. 11.2. Leonard C. Hanna, Jr., Fund. 84.37

Two Kneeling Carthusian Monks. Marble. France, Paris, end 14th c. Max. H. 25.7. John L. Severance Fund. 66.112-.113

Mourner from the Tomb of Duke John the Fearless. Alabaster. Jean de la Huerta, act. Burgundy (b. Spain), 2d quarter 15th c. H. 41. Purchase from the J. H. Wade Fund. 40.129

Prophet (Supporting Figure from the Châsse of Saint-Germain-des-Près). Gilt bronze. France, Paris, ca. 1409. H. 14. Leonard C. Hanna, Jr., Fund. 64.360

John the Baptist. Oil on panel, 1410s. Robert Campin (Master of Flémalle), Netherlandish, Tournai. H. 17.2. Gift of the John Huntington Art and Polytechnic Trust. 66.238

Frontispiece for the Canon of the Mass. From a Missal. Tempera and gold on parchment. Netherlands, Cloister of Agnietenberg near Zwolle, ca. 1438-39. Miniature by Master of Otto van Moerdrecht. H. 33.3. Mr. and Mrs. William H. Marlatt Fund. 59.154

Lavabo. Brass. South Netherlands, 15th c. H. 36.8. Norman O. Stone and Ella A. Stone Memorial Fund. 65.22

John the Baptist in a Landscape. Oil on panel, ca. 1440. Circle of Jan van Eyck, Netherlandish. H. 40.2. Leonard C. Hanna, Jr., Fund. 79.80

Gold Seal of Doge Michele Steno (obverse). Italy, Venice, 1400–1409. D. 4.8. Purchase from the J. H. Wade Fund. 85.198

Initial G with Christ and Virgin in Glory. From an Antiphonary. Tempera and gold on parchment, ca. 1390–1400. Silvestro dei Gherarducci, Italian, Florence. H. 34.9. Purchase from the J. H. Wade Fund. 30.105

Girdle (detail). Silver gilt and translucent enamel. Italy, Siena, late 14th c. Overall L. approx. 236.8. Gift of the John Huntington Art and Polytechnic Trust. 30.742

Mantle for a Figure of the Virgin (detail). Lampas weave; silk and gold. Egypt, Mamluk period, reign of Barsbay(?), 1422–38. Overall H. 111. Purchase from the J. H. Wade Fund. 39.40

Manjusri: Bodhisattva of Wisdom. Gilt bronze. Nepal, 15th c. H. 78.1. Leonard C. Hanna, Jr., Fund. 64.370

Accidia and Her Court. From a *Treatise on Vices.* Ink, tempera, and gold on parchment. Italy, Genoa or Naples(?), late 14th c. H. 19. Purchase from the J. H. Wade Fund. 53.152

Crucifixion with the Two Thieves. Black chalk, pen and brown ink. North Italian, ca. 1425–50. H. 24.4. Delia E. Holden Fund, L. E. Holden Fund, and John L. Severance Fund. 56.43

Madonna of Humility. Tempera on panel, ca. 1400. Attr. to Gherardo Starnina, Italian, act. Florence and Spain. H. 68. Leonard C. Hanna, Jr., Fund. 85.8

The Coronation of the Virgin. From an Antiphonary. Ink, tempera, and gold on parchment. Attr. to Master of the Beffi Triptych, Italian, Tuscany, late 14th c. H. 55.3. Purchase from the J. H. Wade Fund. 53.24

The Madonna of Humility with the Temptation of Eve. Tempera on panel, ca. 1400. Carlo da Camerino, Italian. H. 191.2. Holden Collection. 16.795

Vajravarahi: Dancing Tantric Deity. Dry lacquer. Nepal, 15th c. H. 63.5. Andrew R. and Martha Holden Jennings Fund. 64.103

Madonna and Child. Pen and brown ink. North Italian, ca. 1440. H. 10.7. Delia E. Holden Fund. 56.42

Miniature from a Choral Book: Prophet. Tempera and gold on parchment, ca. 1420. Matteo Torelli, Italian, Florence. H. 16.7. Purchase from the J. H. Wade Fund. 49.536

Spain   **France**   **Italy**

The Coronation of the Virgin.
Tempera on panel, ca. 1400-10.
The Rubielos Master, Spanish.
H. 144.6. Gift of the Hanna
Fund. 47.208

A Bishop Saint with Donor.
Tempera on panel. Spain(?),
ca. 1420. H. 178. Gift of the
Friends of The Cleveland
Museum of Art. 27.197

*Hours of Charles the Noble, Fol.
83r: Presentation in the Temple.*
Ink, tempera, gold on vellum, ca.
1405. Master of Brussels Initials,
Paris. H. 19.4. Mr. and Mrs.
William H. Marlatt Fund. 64.40

*Tondo: The Coronation of the
Virgin.* Embroidery; silk, gold,
and silver. Italy, Florence, ca.
1430-40. D. 57.7. Purchase from
the J. H. Wade Fund. 53.129

Half a Chasuble. Velvet weave,
cut; silk. Italy, early 15th c.
H. 108.5. Purchase from the
J. H. Wade Fund. 43.66

Virgin and Child Enthroned.
Tempera on panel. Master of
1419, Italian, Tuscany. H. 196.2.
Gift of the Hanna Fund. 54.834

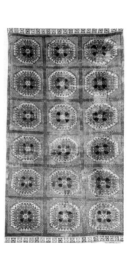

Curtain. Lampas with areas of
compound weave; silk. Spain,
Granada, Nasrid period, 15th c.
H. 438.2. Leonard C. Hanna, Jr.,
Bequest. 82.16

Carpet. Spanish knot; wool.
Spain, Alcarez(?), Mudejar,
2d half 15th c. H. 480.5.
Purchase from the J. H. Wade
Fund. 52.11

*Hours of Charles the Noble,
Fol. 192r: The Deposition.* Ink,
tempera, and gold on vellum, ca.
1405. Egerton Master and Master of Brussels Initials, France,
Paris. H. 19.4. Mr. and Mrs.
William H. Marlatt Fund. 64.40

Textile (detail). Velvet weave,
cut and voided; silk. Italy, 1st
half 15th c. Overall H. 111.5.
Purchase from the J. H. Wade
Fund. 43.67

*Miniature under Initial M: The
Annunciation.* Tempera and
gold on parchment. North
Italian, ca. 1430-40. H. 19.7.
Gift from J. H. Wade. 24.431

St. Francis before the Crucifix.
Tempera on panel, ca. 1440.
Sassetta (Stefano di Giovanni),
Italian, Siena. H. 81. Mr. and
Mrs. William H. Marlatt Fund.
62.36

Half a Chasuble. Velvet weave,
cut, voided; silk. Italy, 15th c.
Orphrey. Embroidery; silk, gold
on linen. Austria, Steiermark(?),
early 15th c. H. 119.3. Purchase
from the J. H. Wade Fund. 50.85

Pata with Four Figures. Color on cloth. Tibet, 15th c. H. 57.8. Purchase from the J. H. Wade Fund. 60.206

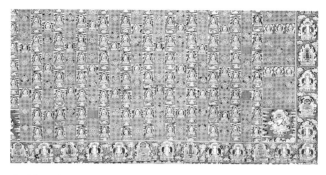

Buddhist Ceremonial Robe (detail). Embroidery; silk and gold. China, early Ming dynasty, beginning of 15th c. Overall W. 299.1. Leonard C. Hanna, Jr., Fund. 87.57

Cupstand. Porcelain with underglaze red decoration. China, Ming dynasty, Hongwu period, 1368-98. D. 22.3. The Severance and Greta Millikin Purchase Fund. 84.162

Buddhist Triptych: Amitabha with Two Attendants. Gilt bronze. Korea, Koryo-Choson periods, 14th-15th c. L. 54.6. The Worcester R. Warner Collection. 18.501

Stem Cup with Animals among Waves. Porcelain with underglaze blue and overglaze red enamel decoration. China, Ming dynasty, Xuande mark and period, 1426-35. H. 8.9. John L. Severance Fund. 57.60

Libation Cup in Form of Wine Warmer (Jue). Glazed porcelain. China, Ming dynasty, Yongle period, 1403-24. H. 15. John L. Severance Fund. 57.59

Mahasiddha Virupa. Gilt bronze. China, Ming dynasty, Yongle mark and period, 1403-24. H. 43.6. Gift of Mary B. Lee, C. Bingham Blossom, Dudley S. Blossom III, Laurel B. Kovacik, and Elizabeth B. Blossom in memory of Elizabeth B. Blossom. 72.96

Landscapes of the Four Seasons. One of a pair of six-fold screens, ink and slight color on paper. Yi Su-mun, Korean, act. ca. 1st half 15th c., Choson period. W. 361.3. John L. Severance Fund. 76.93

Foliate Dish with Grapevines. Porcelain with underglaze blue decoration. China, Ming dynasty, Xuande period, 1426-35. D. 43.2. Anonymous Gift. 53.127

Ritual Disk. Cloisonné enamel. China, Ming dynasty, early 15th c. D. 30.8. Purchase from the J. H. Wade Fund. 87.58

Storage Jar: Punch'ong Ware. Glazed stoneware with incised and stamped decoration. Korea, Choson period, 15th c. H. 37.5. John L. Severance Fund. 63.505

Bottle with Peony Design: Punch'ong Ware. Glazed stoneware. Korea, Choson period, 15-16th c. H. 26.8. The Severance and Greta Millikin Purchase Fund. 90.14

60

Christ Carrying the Cross.
Alabaster. England, Nottingham, 15th c. H. 47. Andrew R.
and Martha Holden Jennings
Fund. 69.296

*Diptych: Four Scenes from
the Passion.* Tempera and oil on
panel, ca. 1400. Austrian
Master, Styria. W. 68.6. Mr. and
Mrs. William H. Marlatt Fund.
45.115

Polyptych: Passion of Christ. Oil
on panel, 1440s. Master of the
Schlägl Altarpiece, German,
Westphalia. W. 210.8. Mr. and
Mrs. William H. Marlatt Fund.
51.453

The Death of the Virgin. Oil on
panel, ca. 1400. Master of Heiligenkreuz, Austria. H. 71. Gift of
Friends of The Cleveland
Museum of Art in memory of
John L. Severance. 36.496

Pietà (Vesperbild). Painted
stone. Austria, Salzburg,
ca. 1400-25. H. 94. Purchase
from the J. H. Wade Fund. 71.67

St. Jerome with the Lion.
Metalcut colored by hand,
ca. 1460-80, state I-II/III.
Germany. H. 35.6. John L.
Severance Fund. 52.13

*St. Augustine and the Child
on the Seashore.* Engraving,
ca. 1465-69, unique. Master of
the Nuremberg Passion, German. H. 19.1. Leonard C. Hanna,
Jr., Fund. 84.55

The Coronation of the Virgin.
Tempera on panel, early 15th c.
Master of the Fröndenberg
Altarpiece, German, Westphalia. H. 67.6. Gift of Friends of
The Cleveland Museum of Art.
29.920

The Adoration of the Magi. Oil
on panel, mid 15th c. Konrad
Laib, Austrian. H. 100. Delia E.
and L. E. Holden Funds. 36.18

Samson Rending the Lion.
Engraving, 1460-67. Master
E. S., German. H. 12.3. Grace
Rainey Rogers Fund. 48.456

*An Angel Supporting Two
Escutcheons.* Black chalk.
Lower Rhenish school, ca. 1470.
W. 21.2. Dudley P. Allen Fund
and Delia E. Holden Fund.
62.205

Initial with Miniature: Virgin as Queen of Heaven. Ink, tempera, and gold on parchment. Italy, Milan(?), 2d quarter 15th c. H. 56.2. Purchase from the J. H. Wade Fund. 28.652

Oak-Leaf Jar. Maiolica, ca. 1430, Workshop of Giunta di Tugio, Italian, Florence. H. 20.4. Purchase from the J. H. Wade Fund. 43.54

Bookbinding. Leather chased and perforated over gold. Iran, Timurid period, 15th c. H. 35.9. Purchase from the J. H. Wade Fund. 44.495

The Hermit Xu You Resting by a Stream. Hanging scroll, ink and slight color on silk. Dai Jin, Chinese, 1388-1462, Ming dynasty. H. 138. John L. Severance Fund. 74.45

Bodhisattvas of the Ten Stages of Enlightenment. Hanging scroll, ink and color on silk, dated 1454. China, Ming dynasty. H. 141. John L. Severance Fund. 73.70

Medal: John VIII Palaeologus, Emperor of Constantinople 1425-28. Lead. Antonio Pisano (called Pisanello), Italian, Pisa, ca. 1395-Rome 1455. D. 10.4. John L. Severance Fund. 74.109

Medal: Leonello d'Este, Marquess of Ferrara. Bronze, ca. 1440-44. Antonio di Puccio Pisano (called Pisanello), Italian. D. 6.9. Andrew R. and Martha Holden Jennings Fund. 71.4

Courtly Scene. Frontispiece from *Shanamah of Firdawsi.* Opaque watercolor and silver on paper. Iran, Shiraz, Timurid period, ca. 1444. H. 26.7. John L. Severance Fund. 56.10

A Demon in Chains. From an album in Istanbul. Opaque watercolor and gold on paper. Attr. to Muhammad Siyah-Qalam, Iran or Central Asia, 15th c. W. 35.2. Purchase from the J. H. Wade Fund. 82.63

Daoist Immortal Li Tieguai. Bronze. Su Wennan, Chinese, 15th c., Ming dynasty. H. 41.8. Cornelia Blakemore Warner Fund. 73.158

Bowl with Lily Scroll. Porcelain with underglaze blue decoration. China, Ming dynasty, Chenghua mark and period, 1465-87. D. 14.5. Gift of John D. Rockefeller, III and John L. Severance Fund. 67.64

Navicella. Pen and brown ink, ca. 1430. Attr. to Parri Spinelli, Italian. W. 37.1. Purchase from the J. H. Wade Fund. 61.38

Plate. Maiolica, inscribed: *Maria.* Spain, Valencia, Hispano-Moresque, mid 15th c. D. 46.7. Purchase from the J. H. Wade Fund. 44.292

Biblia Pauperum: Fols. I and K Woodcut colored by hand, mid 15th c. Netherlands. W. 39.2. John L. Severance Fund. 86.91

Adoration of the Magi. Tempera and oil on panel, ca. 1440. Giovanni di Paolo, Italian, Siena. W. 46.2. Delia E. and L. E. Holden Funds. 42.536

Chest. Painted wood. Spain, Catalan(?), late 15th c. H. 71.7. Gift of the John Huntington Art and Polytechnic Trust. 15.535

John the Baptist. Oil on panel, 1450s. Dieric Bouts, Netherlandish. H. 106. Gift of the Hanna Fund. 51.354

The Adoration of the Magi. Oil on panel, 1480s. Geertgen tot Sint Jans, Netherlandish. H. 29.2. Gift of the Hanna Fund. 51.353

St. Anthony Abbot. Tempera on panel, 1457. Filippo Lippi, Italian, Florence. H. 81.3. Leonard C. Hanna, Jr., Fund. 64.151

St. Michael. Tempera on panel, 1457. Filippo Lippi, Italian, Florence. H. 81.3. Leonard C. Hanna, Jr., Fund. 64.150

Birth and Naming of John the Baptist. Oil on panel, ca. 1510. Juan de Flandes, Hispano-Flemish. H. 88.4. John L. Severance Fund. 75.3

The Annunciation. Oil on panel, ca. 1480. Aelbrecht Bouts, Netherlandish. H. 50.2. Bequest of John L. Severance. 42.635

Chapel de Fer (Helmet). Steel. Missaglia workshop, Italy, Milan, ca. 1475. L. 36.2. Gift of Mr. and Mrs. John L. Severance. 16.1565

St. Catherine of Siena and the Beggar. Tempera on panel, mid 15th c. Giovanni di Paolo, Italian, Siena. W. 28.9. Gift of the John Huntington Art and Polytechnic Trust. 66.3

River Village in a Rainstorm. Hanging scroll, ink and slight color on silk. Lu Wenying, Chinese, act. late 15th c., Ming dynasty. H. 169.2. John L. Severance Fund. 70.76

A Pair of Peacocks. Hanging scroll, ink on silk. Lin Liang, Chinese, act. ca. 1450-1500, Ming dynasty. H. 154. Severance and Greta Millikin Collection. 64.242

Winter and Spring Landscape. Six-fold screen, ink and slight color on paper. Attr. to Shubun, Japanese, ca. 1414-63, Muromachi period. W. 265.8. The Norweb Collection. 58.476

Portrait of a Man. Oil on panel, mid 15th c. Colantonio(?), Italian, Naples. H. 60. Holden Collection. 16.811

The Poet Lin Bu Wandering in the Moonlight. Hanging scroll, ink and slight color on paper. Du Jin, Chinese, act. ca. 1465-1505, Ming dynasty. H. 156.5. John L. Severance Fund. 54.582

Daoist Immortal Zhongli Quan. Hanging scroll, ink and color on silk. Zhao Qi, Chinese, act. ca. 1488-1505, Ming dynasty. H. 134.5. Purchase from the J. H. Wade Fund. 76.13

Writing Box. Lacquer on wood with *maki-e* lacquer design. Japan, Muromachi period, 15th c. W. 24.2. John L. Severance Fund. 69.124

Windy Landscape. Hanging scroll, ink on paper. Japan, Muromachi period, 15th c. H. 84.6. John L. Severance Fund. 82.131

Noh Mask of Okina. Polychromed wood with hemp. Japan, Muromachi period, 15th c. H. 20.3. Purchase from the J. H. Wade Fund. 77.33

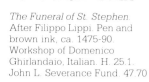

The Funeral of St. Stephen. After Filippo Lippi. Pen and brown ink, ca. 1475-90. Workshop of Domenico Ghirlandaio, Italian. H. 25.1. John L. Severance Fund. 47.70

Storage Jar: Echizen Ware. Stoneware with natural ash glaze. Japan, Muromachi period, 15th c. H. 49.8. John L. Severance Fund. 89.70

Kettle with Crane Design. Cast iron. Japan, Muromachi period, 15th c. H. 31.3. Purchase from the J. H. Wade Fund. 80.11

Tunic. Interlocked tapestry with embroidered edge; wool and cotton. Peru, South Coast, Ica Valley(?), Inca culture, ca. 1400-1532. H. 83.1. Gift of William R. Carlisle. 57.136

Miniature Showing Queen Medusa Enthroned. Tempera on parchment. France, close to Maître François, ca. 1470. H. 12.7. Gift from J. H. Wade. 24.1015

Madonna and Child with Saints. Tapestry weave; wool, silk, and linen. Germany, Nuremberg, ca. 1470-75. W. 156.1. Gift of Leonard C. Hanna, Jr., for the

Coralie Walker Hanna Memorial Collection. 39.162

Madonna and Child. From Ciborium of Cardinal d'Estouteville in S. Maria Maggiore, Rome. Marble, ca. 1461-64. Mino del Reame(?), Italian. H. 93.7. Gift of Mrs. Leonard C. Hanna. 28.747

Head of a Boy. Marble. Italy, Florence, ca. 1470. H. 24.3. Purchase from the J. H. Wade Fund. 31.454

Portrait of a Man. Oil on panel, ca. 1490-1500. French Master. H. 42.5. Leonard C. Hanna, Jr., Fund. 63.503

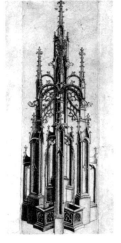

Design for a Gothic Fountain. Engraving, ca. 1470. Master W with a Key, Flemish. H. 23.3. Dudley P. Allen Fund. 37.565

Monstrance with Relic of St. Sebastian. From Guelph Treasure. Silver gilt and crystal. Germany, Lower Saxony, Brunswick(?), 2d half 15th c. H. 17. Gift of Julius F. Goldschmidt, Z. M. Hackenbroch, and J. Rosenbaum in Memory of the Exhibition of the Guelph Treasure Held in The Cleveland Museum of Art from January 10 to February 1, 1931. 31.65

Madonna and Child. Painted terracotta, ca. 1475. Antonio Rossellino and workshop, Italian, Florence. H. 91.4. Bequest of John L. Severance. 42.780

Adoration of the Christ Child. Marble with gilding. Workshop of Benedetto Briosco and Tommaso Cazzaniga, Italian, Lombardy, late 15th c. H. 61. Gift of the John Huntington Art and Polytechnic Trust. 28.863

Front Cover for a Gospel Book of Cardinal Jean Balue. Silver, silver gilt, and niello. Italy, Florence, ca. 1467-68. H. 41.6. Purchase from the J. H. Wade Fund. 52.109

Adoration of the Shepherds. Leaf from an Antiphonary. Ink, tempera, and gold on parchment, ca. 1470. Italy, Siena, H. 57.2. Purchase from the J. H. Wade Fund. 52.282

Miniature: Pietà. Tempera on parchment. Attr. to Andrea Mantegna, Italian, 1431-1506. H. 14.1. Purchase from the J. H. Wade Fund. 51.394

Garden Scene. Opaque watercolor on paper (unfinished). Iran, Herat, Timurid period, style of Bihzad, ca. 1485. H. 26.4. Edward L. Whittemore Fund. 44.490

Buddhist Offering Figure. Embroidery; silk and gold. Central Asia, Chinese Turkestan, ca. 2d quarter 15th c. H. 65.6. John L. Severance Fund. 87.145

Cloud-Climbing Pavilion. From *Twelve Views of Tiger Hill.* Album leaf, ink and slight color on paper. Shen Zhou, Chinese, 1427-1509, Ming dynasty. W. 20.2. Leonard C. Hanna, Jr., Fund. 64.371

Initial M. From a Gradual. Tempera and gold on parchment. Attr. to Cosimo Tura, Italian, Ferrara, 1432-95. H. 76.8. Purchase from the J. H. Wade Fund. 27.425

Tabernacle. Polychromed marble. North Italian, late 15th c. H. 81.3. Purchase from the J. H. Wade Fund. 75.105

Hundred Birds Admiring the Peacocks. Hanging scroll, ink and color on silk. Yin Hong, Chinese, late 15th-early 16th c., Ming dynasty. H. 240. Purchase from the J. H. Wade Fund. 74.31

Holy Trinity. Oil on panel, 1470s. French Master, Provence(?). H. 119. Mr. and Mrs. William H. Marlatt Fund. 60.79

Hours of Queen Isabella the Catholic of Spain, Fols. 72v and 73r: The Crucifixion and Deposition. Ink, tempera, and gold on vellum. Flanders, ca. 1492-97. L. 22.6. Leonard C. Hanna, Jr., Fund. 63.256

The Mystical Grapes. Tapestry weave; wool, silk, and metallic threads. Netherlands, ca. 1500. H. 73.3. John L. Severance Fund. 73.77

Chalice and Paten. Gilt silver and filigree enamel. Hungary, 2d half 15th c. *Chalice*: H. 25. John L. Severance Fund. 90.3-.4

A Bridal Pair. Oil on panel, ca. 1470. South German Master. H. 64.7. Delia E. and L. E. Holden Funds. 32.179

Triptych. Onyx cameo. Italy, 13th c. Gold and translucent enamel. France, late 15th c. H. 5.7. Purchase from the J. H. Wade Fund. 47.508

A Monk at Prayer. Oil on panel, early 16th c. Netherlandish Master, Bruges. H. 37.5. John L. Severance Collection. 42.632

Lady with Three Suitors. Pen and brown ink, brown wash, over traces of black chalk. France, ca. 1500. H. 23. John L. Severance Fund. 56.40

Scenes from the Childhood of Christ. Tapestry weave; wool, silk, and gold metallic threads. Franco-Flemish, Hainaut, late 15th-early 16th c. W. 233.7. Bequest of John L. Severance. 42.826

Paternoster Bead. Boxwood. Flanders, early 16th c. H. 5.7. Purchase from the J. H. Wade Fund. 61.87

St. Andrew. Oak with traces of paint. North Netherlands, ca. 1520. H. 70.8. Gift of John D. Rockefeller, Jr. 28.169

Angel Playing Lute. Polychromed wood, ca. 1503. Hans Schnatterpeck, Austrian, South Tyrol. H. 74.9. Gift of Severance and Greta Millikin. 59.340

Medallion: Annunciation. Ivory. Germany, Upper Rhine, end 15th c. D. 7. Andrew R. and Martha Holden Jennings Fund. 71.7

Pedlar Goblet. Enameled glass. Italy, Venice, ca. 1475. H. 18.9. Purchase from the J. H. Wade Fund. 53.364

Drug Bottle. Maiolica. Italy, Faenza, ca. 1480. H. 38.7. Purchase from the J. H. Wade Fund. 43.52

Marriage Beaker. Enameled milk glass. Italy, Venice, late 15th c. H. 10.2. Purchase from the J. H. Wade Fund. 57.50

Plate. Maiolica. Italy, Faenza, late 15th c. D. 35.6. Gift from J. H. Wade. 23.915

Horses and Grooms in the Stable (detail). One of a pair of six-fold screens, ink and color on paper. Japan, Muromachi period, 1392-1573. Overall W. 348.6. Edward L. Whittemore Fund. 34.374

Head of a Man (verso). Metalpoint on purple prepared paper, ca. 1450-60. Workshop of Benozzo Gozzoli, Italian. H. 19.4. Purchase from the J. H. Wade Fund. 37.24

Tarocchi Cards: Logic. Engraving, colored by hand with gold, ca. 1465. Master of the E-series Tarocchi, Italian. H. 18.2. Dudley P. Allen Fund. 24.453

The Risen Christ Between SS. Andrew and Longinus. Engraving, ca. 1472. Andrea Mantegna, Italian. H. 30.5. Gift in memory of Mildred Andrews Putnam. 86.103

St. Christopher. Pen and brown ink with blue and green washes, touches of white, ca. 1460-70. Circle of Andrea Mantegna, Italian. H. 28.7. Dudley P. Allen Fund. 56.39

Hotei. Hanging scroll, ink on paper. Inscription by Jonan Etetsu. Japan, Muromachi period, late 15th c. H. 51. Mr. and Mrs. William H. Marlatt Fund. 88.17

Monk in a Landscape. Hanging scroll, ink on paper. Ikkyu Sojun, Japanese, 1394-1481, Muromachi period. H. 76.8. Mr. and Mrs. William H. Marlatt Fund. 85.89

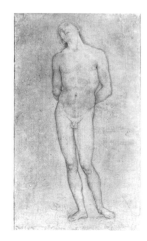

Battle of The Nudes. Engraving, ca. 1470-75, state I/II, unique. Antonio Pollaiuolo, Italian. W. 61.1. Purchase from the J. H. Wade Fund. 67.127

St. Sebastian. Pen and brown ink over metalpoint on gray prepared paper, ca. 1490. Pietro Perugino, Italian. H. 25.6. Dudley P. Allen Fund. 58.411

View of the Xiao and Xiang Rivers. Fusuma panel remounted as a hanging scroll, ink on paper, ca. 1509. Soami, Japanese, Muromachi period. H. 128.6. John L. Severance Fund. 63.262

Adoration of The Magi.
Engraving, 1513, state I/III.
Lucas van Leyden, Netherlandish. W. 43.2. The Charles W.
Harkness Endowment Fund.
23.274

The Bearing of the Cross.
Engraving, 1470-90. Martin
Schongauer, German. W. 43.4.
Dudley P. Allen Fund. 41.389

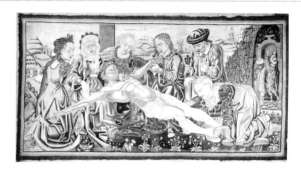

The Lamentation. Tapestry
weave; wool, silk, gold, and
silver. Italy, Ferrara, after design
by Cosimo Tura, ca. 1475.
W. 197. John L. Severance
Fund. 50.145

Samson and Delilah. Woodcut,
ca. 1512. Lucas van Leyden,
Netherlandish. H. 41.3. Gift of
The Print Club of Cleveland in
memory of Charles T. Brooks.
35.117

The Organ Player and His Wife.
Engraving, state I/III. Israhel van
Meckenem, German, before
1450-1503. H. 16.7. Delia E.
Holden Fund. 60.73

*The Apocalypse: The Four
Horsemen.* Woodcut, ca.
1497/8, proof before text. H. 39.
Albrecht Dürer, German. Gift of
The Print Club of Cleveland.
32.313

*Portrait of a Youth as St.
Sebastian.* Oil on panel, 1490s.
Ambrogio de Predis, Italian,
Milan. H. 31.7. John L.
Severance Fund. 86.9

*Portrait of a Novice of the Order
of San Secondo.* Oil on panel,
late 15th c. Jacometto Veneziano, Italian, Venice. H. 24.1.
Mr. and Mrs. William H. Marlatt
Fund. 76.9

The Nativity. Oil on panel, ca.
1490. Gerard David, Netherlandish. H. 85.2. Leonard C. Hanna,
Jr., Fund. 58.320

*The Virgin and Child with a
Monkey.* Engraving, ca. 1498.
Albrecht Dürer, German.
H. 19.1. Dudley P. Allen Fund.
64.29

Christ on the Mount of Olives.
Etching on iron plate, 1515.
Albrecht Dürer, German.
H. 22.3. Purchase from the
J. H. Wade Fund. 43.389

*Mother and Child with Two
Dogs.* Engraving. Italian, late
15th c. H. 14.9. Dudley P. Allen
Fund. 37.566

*Virgin and Child with a
Goldfinch.* Tempera(?) on panel,
ca. 1495. Neroccio de'Landi,
Italian, Siena. H. 38.8. Leonard
C. Hanna, Jr., Fund. 80.101

The Crucifixion. Tempera on panel, ca 1480. Matteo di Giovanni di Bartolo, Italian, Siena. W. 31. Bequest of James Parmelee. 40.535

Scholar-Hermits in the Autumn Mountains (detail). Handscroll, ink and slight color on silk. Tang Yin, Chinese, 1470-1523, Ming dynasty. Overall W. 232.4.

Andrew R. and Martha Holden Jennings Fund. 76.94

Virgin and Child. Tempera(?) on panel, ca. 1470. Francesco Botticini, Italian, Florence. H. 96.7. Holden Collection. 16.789

St. Nicholas of Bari. Oil on panel, 1472. Carlo Crivelli, Italian, Venice. H. 97.3. Gift of the Hanna Fund. 52.111

The Assumption of the Virgin. After Sandro Botticelli. Engraving on 2 sheets, ca. 1490-95, state I/II. Francesco Rosselli, Italian. H. 81.6. Purchase from the J. H. Wade Fund. 49.32

St. Jerome in Penitence. Engraving, ca. 1480-1500. Italian. W. 21.5. Dudley P. Allen Fund. 49.33

Virgin and Child with SS. Anthony Abbot, Sebastian, Mark, and Severino. Tempera(?) on panel, 1490s. Lorenzo d'Alessandro da Sanseverino, Italian, Umbria. H. 128.9. Holden Collection. 16.800

Plum Blossoms. Hanging scroll, ink on silk. Peng Xu, Chinese, act. ca. 1488-1521, Ming dynasty. H. 127. John L. Severance Fund. 70.80

The Last Supper. After Perugino. Engraving on 2 sheets, ca. 1500. Lucantonio degli Uberti, Italian. W. 53.3. Dudley P. Allen Fund. 40.473-a

View of a Castle. Pen and brown ink, 1513. Wolfgang Huber, Austrian. W. 21.2. John L. Severance Fund. 51.277

Gospel Book. Ink, tempera, and gold on parchment. Germany, Middle Rhine, ca. 1480. Miniatures by Master of the Hausbuch. Contemporary leather binding. H. 22.9. Mr. and Mrs. William H. Marlatt Fund. 52.465

Time. Tapestry weave; wool and silk. France, 1500-10. W. 439.7. Leonard C. Hanna, Jr., Bequest. 60.178

SS. Lawrence and Stephen. Lindenwood, 1502-10. Tilmann Riemenschneider, German. Max. H. 94.6. Leonard C. Hanna, Jr., Fund. 59.42-.43

Abbot's Stall. Oak. France, 1500-15. H. approx. 324.4. Purchase from the J. H. Wade Fund. 28.657

Head of a Woman. Silverpoint on buff prepared paper. Hans Holbein I, German, ca. 1465-1524. H. 65. Purchase from the J. H. Wade Fund. 70.14

Virgin and Child with the Young John the Baptist. Tempera on panel, ca. 1490. Sandro Botticelli and Workshop, Italian, Florence. D. 68. Leonard C. Hanna, Jr., Fund. 70.160

The Holy Family with the Young John the Baptist and St. Margaret. Tempera and oil on panel, ca. 1495. Filippino Lippi, Italian, Florence. D. 153. Purchase from the Delia E. Holden Fund and from a fund donated as a memorial to Mrs. Holden by her children: Guerdon S. Holden, Delia Holden White, Roberta Holden Bole, Emery Holden Greenough, Gertrude Holden McGinley. 32.227

Miniature: Christ on the Mt. of Olives. Tempera on parchment, ca. 1490-1500. Attr. to Timoteo Viti, Italian, Umbria. H. 27. Purchase from the J. H. Wade Fund. 27.161

Crucified Christ. Bronze. Severo Calzetta da Ravenna, Italian, act. Padua, ca. 1500. H. 28.6. John L. Severance Fund. 82.127

Haboku (Flung-Ink) Land-scape. Hanging scroll, ink on paper. Shugetsu, Japanese, d. ca. 1510, Muromachi period. H. 59.5. Purchase from the J. H. Wade Fund. 76.59

Mourning Virgin from a Crucifixion Group. Pearwood, 1500-10. Veit Stoss, German. H. 31.4. Purchase from the J. H. Wade Fund. 39.64

Bird's-Eye View of Venice (detail). Woodcut on 6 sheets, 1500, state I/III. Jacopo de' Barbari, Italian. W. 284.5. Purchase from the J. H. Wade Fund. 49.565-.570

Venus Reclining in a Land-scape. After Giorgione. Engraving, ca. 1508/09, state I/II. W. 18.3. Giulio Campagnola, Italian. Gift of The Print Club of Cleveland. 31.205

The Submersion of Pharaoh's Army in the Red Sea (detail). Woodcut on 12 sheets, ca. 1514/5 (printed 1549). Titian, Italian. Overall W. 221.6. John L. Severance Fund. 52.296-.307

Ewer. "Chalcedony" glass. Italy, Venice, ca. 1500. H. 29.6. John L. Severance Fund. 85.141

Water-Moon Kannon. Hanging scroll, ink on paper. Attr. to Gakuo, Japanese, late 15th-early 16th c., Muromachi period. H. 104.5. John L. Severance Fund. 85.110

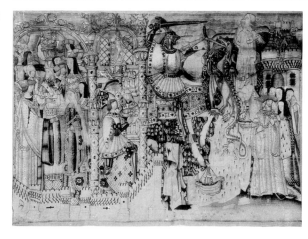

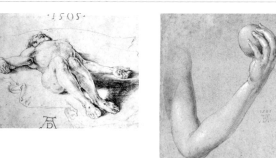

The Dead Christ. Charcoal, 1505. Albrecht Dürer, German. W. 23.5. Gift of the Hanna Fund. 52.531

Arm of Eve. Brush and brown and white ink, 1507. Albrecht Dürer, German. H. 33.6. Accessions Reserve Fund. 65.470

Emperor Maximilian. Woodcut printed in black and white ink on blue tinted paper, 1508, state I/VII, unique. Hans Burgkmair, German. H. 32.1. John L. Severance Fund. 50.72

Perseus and Andromeda. Tapestry weave; wool and silk. South Netherlands, Flanders, early 16th c. W. 446.7. Gift of the John Huntington Art and Polytechnic Trust. 27.487

The Ascension. Pen and brown ink, ca. 1515. H. 31.1. Albrecht Dürer, German. Gift of the Hanna Fund. 52.530

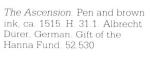

Pyramus and Thisbe. Chiaroscuro woodcut, ca. 1515. Hans Wechtlin, German. H. 27.1. John L. Severance Fund. 50.396

Salome with the Head of John the Baptist. Pen and black ink heightened with white, 1517(?). Albrecht Altdorfer, German. H. 19.2. John L. Severance Fund. 48.440

The Fall and Redemption of Man. Four woodcuts, ca. 1515, uncut proof sheet. Albrecht Altdorfer, German. H. ea. 7.1. John L. Severance Fund. 52.70-.73

Landscape with John the Baptist Preaching. Oil on panel, ca. 1540. Herri met de Bles, Netherlandish. W. 42. Andrew R. and Martha Holden Jennings Fund. 67.20

Christ Child. Marble, ca. 1490-1500. Attr. to Michele di Luca Marini, Italian. H. 87.6. In memory of Leonard C. Hanna, Jr., Gift of Mr. and Mrs. Germain Seligman, New York. 75.47

Pomona. Bronze, ca. 1500. Andrea Briosco (called Riccio), Italian, Padua. H. 15.5. Gift of Mr. and Mrs. Severance A. Millikin. 48.486

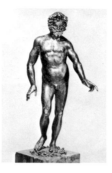

Standing Figure of a Man. Bronze, ca. 1500, Circle of Francesco di Giorgio, Italian, Siena. H. 31. John L. Severance Fund. 47.509

St. John. Terracotta. Master of the Statuettes of St. John, Italian, Florence, act. ca. 1490-1525. H. 72.1. John L. Severance Fund. Bequest of John L. Severance. 42.781

Textile. Lampas weave; silk. Iran, Herat, Safavid period, early 16th c. H. 83.5. Purchase from the J. H. Wade Fund. 24.743

Winter Landscape. Hanging scroll, ink and slight color on silk. Korea, Choson period, 14th-15th c. H. 92.2. John L. Severance Fund. 86.45

Philoctetes on the Island of Lemnos. Marble. Antonio Lombardo, Italian, Padua or Venice, ca. 1438-1516(?). H. 23.3. Purchase from the J. H. Wade Fund. 73.168

Leaf from a Book of Hours: Annunciation. Tempera and gold on vellum. Attr. to Attavante degli Attavanti, Italian, Florence, 1452-1520/25. H. 15.2. Purchase from the J. H. Wade Fund. 53.280

Plaque: Adoration of the Magi. Bronze, ca. 1500-1506. Andrea Briosco (called Riccio), Italian, Padua. W. 31.9. John L. Severance Fund. 54.601

Mihrab and Frieze (detail). Faience mosaic tiles. Iran, Isfahan, Safavid period, 1st half 16th c. Overall H. 290.8. Gift of Katherine Holden Thayer. 62.23

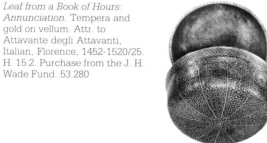

Altarpiece: Madonna and Child Enthroned with SS. Francis and Anthony Abbot. Tin-glazed earthenware, 1510-20. Benedetto Buglioni, Italian, Florence. H. 200. Gift from J. H. Wade. 21.1180

Bowl Ornamented with Damascene Patterns. Bronze inlaid with gold and silver. Italy, Venice, early 16th c. D. 13.2. Purchase from the J. H. Wade Fund. 45.133

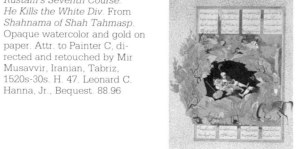

Rustam's Seventh Course: He Kills the White Div. From *Shahnama of Shah Tahmasp.* Opaque watercolor and gold on paper. Attr. to Painter C, directed and retouched by Mir Musavvir, Iranian, Tabriz, 1520s-30s. H. 47. Leonard C. Hanna, Jr., Bequest. 88.96

Bamboo in Moonlight. Hanging scroll, ink on paper. Korea, Choson period, 15th-16th c. H. 85.5. Andrew R. and Martha Holden Jennings Fund. 87.186

Seated Figure. Soapstone. Africa, Sierra Leone, Sape, ca. 16th c. H. 23.8. Gift of Lucile Munro in memory of her husband, Thomas Munro, Curator of Education from 1931 to 1967. 76.29

Head of a Man and Woman. Marble. France, Touraine, Circle of Michel Colombe, 2d decade 16th c. Max. H. 14.6. Gift of William G. Mather. 21.1003-.1004

Education of the Virgin. Limestone. France, Bourbonnais, early 16th c. H. 137.7. Gift of G. J. Demotte. 23.51

Adoration of the Shepherds. Engraving, ca. 1522-25. Frans Crabbe, Flemish. H. 24.6. Purchase from the J. H. Wade Fund. 66.121

The Vision of St. Bernard. Engraving, 1524. Dirk Vellert, Netherlandish. H. 17.1. Dudley P. Allen Fund. 47.118

Stained Glass Panel: Esther before Ahasuerus. Ca. 1530. Attr. to Dirk Vellert, Netherlandish. H. 69.3. John L. Severance Fund. 68.189

Stained Glass Panel: The Judgment of Solomon. Ca. 1530. Attr. to Dirk Vellert, Netherlandish. H. 69.3. John L. Severance Fund. 69.188

St. Jerome and the Lion. Alabaster, end 15th c. Tilmann Riemenschneider, German. H. 37.8. Purchase from the J. H. Wade Fund. 46.82

Helmet in the Maximilian Style. Steel. Germany, early 16th c. H. 30.5. Gift of Mr. and Mrs. John L. Severance. 16.1855

The Mass of St. Gregory. Oil on panel, 1511. Hans Baldung (called Grien), German. W. 124.9. Gift of the Hanna Fund. 52.112

Plaque: Christ in the Garden of Gethsemane. Kelheim stone, ca. 1515. Adolph Daucher, German, Augsburg. H. 14.8. Purchase from the J. H. Wade Fund. 47.182

Adam and Eve. Bronze, dated 1515 (the model), on reverse 1518 (the cast). Ludwig Krug, German, Nuremberg. H. 12.2. John L. Severance Fund. 48.359

Battle in a Wood. Engraving and drypoint, early 16th c. Master of the Year 1515, act. in Italy. W. 32. Dudley P. Allen Fund. 49.34

Farm on the Slope of a Hill. Pen and brown ink, ca. 1508. Fra Bartolommeo, Italian. W. 29.4. Gift of the Hanna Fund. Purchase, Dudley P. Allen Fund,

Delia E. Holden Fund, and L. E. Holden Fund. 57.498

Beggars and Street Characters (detail). Handscroll, ink and color on paper, dated 1516. Zhou Chen, Chinese, Ming dynasty. Overall W. 244.5. John L. Severance Fund. 64.94

Study Sheet. Metalpoint on pink prepared paper, ca. 1506-11. Raphael (Raffaello Sanzio), Italian. W. 15.3. Purchase from the J. H. Wade Fund. 78.37

Virgin and Child with SS. Anthony Abbot and Lucy(?) with Donors. Oil on panel, ca. 1515. Giovanni Battista Cima da Conegliano, Italian, Venice.

W. 80. Bequest of John L. Severance. 42.636

The Garden for Self-Enjoyment (detail). Handscroll, ink and color on silk. Qiu Ying, Chinese, 1494-1552, Ming dynasty. Overall W. 381. John L. Severance Fund. 78.67

Portrait of a Man. Oil on panel, 1510s. Bartolommeo Veneto, Italian, Venice. H. 39.4. Bequest of James Parmelee. 40.539

The Sacrifice of Isaac. Oil on panel, ca. 1527. Andrea del Sarto, Italian, Florence. H. 178.2. Delia E. and L. E. Holden Funds. 37.577

Apollo on Parnassus. After Raphael. Engraving, ca. 1517-20, before state I/II, unique. W. 47.1. Marcantonio Raimondi, Italian. Gift of The Print Club of Cleveland. 63.231

Flowers of Four Seasons (detail). Handscroll, ink and slight color on silk, dated 1531. Wang Guxiang, Chinese, Ming dynasty. Overall W. 545. John L. Severance Fund. 77.4

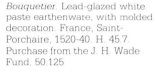

Adam and Eve. Bronze, ca. 1520. Workshop of Peter Vischer the Younger, German, Nuremberg. H. 14.6. Norman O. Stone and Ella A. Stone Memorial Fund. 61.29

Pietà (Vesperbild). Lindenwood, painted and gilded, ca. 1515-30. Master of Rabenden, German, Bavaria, Chiemgau. H. 89.1. Purchase from the J. H. Wade Fund. 38.294

Corpus of Christ. Lindenwood, ca. 1525-30. Hans Leinberger, German, Bavaria, Landshut. H. 118.1. Purchase from the J. H. Wade Fund. 38.293

Plate: The Three Graces. Maiolica, 1525. Maestro Giorgio (Giorgio Andreoli da Gubbio), Italian, Gubbio. D. 44.8. Purchase from the J. H. Wade Fund. 45.2

Plate. Maiolica, signed: *M. G. da Agubio,* dated 1526. Maestro Giorgio (Giorgio Andreoli da Gubbio), Italian. D. 17. Purchase from the J. H. Wade Fund. 50.156

Bouquetier. Lead-glazed white paste earthenware, with molded decoration. France, Saint-Porchaire, 1520-40. H. 45.7. Purchase from the J. H. Wade Fund. 50.125

Adam and Eve. Boxwood. Attr. to Daniel Mauch, German, 1477-1540. H. 22.2. Purchase from the J. H. Wade Fund. 46.429

Model for a Medal: Son of Martin III Geuder. Kelheim stone, dated 1528. Matthes Gebel, German, Nuremberg. D. 3.7. John L. Severance Fund. 56.25

Portrait of Wolfgang Gamensfelder. Boxwood, dated 1531. Master of Gamensfelder and Fronleitner, German. D. 11.9. Andrew R. and Martha Holden Jennings Fund. 76.16

Plate. Maiolica. Italy, Deruta, early 16th c. D. 41.3. Gift from J. H. Wade. 23.1096

Bowl with St. Francis Receiving the Stigmata. Maiolica, dated 1531. Italy, Deruta. D. 41.3. Gift of the Mildred Andrews Fund. 88.95

Plaque: The Trojan Horse. Painted enamel, ca. 1530-40. Master of the Aeneid Series, France, Limoges. H. 23.8. Andrew R. and Martha Holden Jennings Fund. 74.40

Sitting Dog. Bronze. South Germany or Austria (Innsbruck), 2d quarter 16th c. H. 5.9. Purchase from the J. H. Wade Fund. 60.74

Fountain Figure of Abundance. Bronze, ca. 1530-40. Master of the Budapest Abundance, German, Augsburg. H. 36.8. Purchase from the J. H. Wade Fund. 71.104

Plate: The Prodigal Son. After Dürer. Maiolica, signed and dated 1528. Maestro Giorgio (Giorgio Andreoli da Gubbio), Gubbio. D. 21.2. Purchase from the J. H. Wade Fund. 50.82

Albarello. Maiolica. Italy, Faenza, early 16th c. H. 29.8. Purchase from the J. H. Wade Fund. 40.12

Nanda and the Elders. From the *Bhagavata Purana.* Color on paper. India, Rajasthan, Mewar school, ca. 1525-50. H. 22.8. Mr. and Mrs. William H. Marlatt Fund. 60.53

Woman (Thetis?). Bronze. Italy, Padua, ca. 1527. H. 18.2. Norman O. Stone and Ella A. Stone Memorial Fund. 63.92

Madonna and Child. Bronze, signed ca. 1527. Jacopo Tatti (called Sansovino), Italian. H. 47.6. John L. Severance Fund. 51.316

Venus Prudentia. Gilt bronze. Attr. to Tullio Lombardo, Italian, Venice, ca. 1455-1532. H. 18.3. John L. Severance Fund. 48.171

Plaque: Satyress. Bronze, ca. 1520-30. Andrea Briosco (called Riccio), Italian, Padua. H. 16.5. Gift of Mr. and Mrs. Severance A. Millikin. 47.29

Pastiglia Casket. White lead pastiglia decoration on gilt alder. Italy, Venice, 1st half 16th c. L. 29.9. John L. Severance Fund. 81.8

Figure of Plenty (Dovizia). Glazed terracotta, early 16th c. Giovanni della Robbia, Italian. H. 110.2. Gift of S. Livingston Mather, Constance Mather Bishop, Philip R. Mather, Katherine Hoyt Cross, and Katherine Mather McLean in accordance with the wishes of Samuel Mather. 40.343

St. Margaret. Marble, 1520-30. Antonello Gagini, Italian, Sicily. H. 139.7. Purchase from the J. H. Wade Fund. 42.564

Toad. Bronze. Italy, Padua(?), 1st half 16th c. L. 13. The Severance and Greta Millikin Purchase Fund. 87.5

France **Netherlands** **Germany**

Hat Jewel: Adoration of the Magi. Enamel on gold. France, mid 16th c. D. 4.7. Purchase from the J. H. Wade Fund. 38.428

Christ Carrying the Cross. Alabaster, ca. 1545. Workshop of Jacques du Broeucq, South Netherlands, Hainaut. H. 61.1. Purchase from the J. H. Wade Fund. 71.5

Double Mazer. Maple with gilt-silver mounts. Germany, ca. 1530. Portrait medallion (1528) by Matthes Gebel, Nuremberg. H. 24.8. Purchase from the J. H. Wade Fund. 50.83

Terminus: The Device of Erasmus of Rotterdam. Oil on panel, ca. 1530. Hans Holbein the Younger, German. H. 21.6. Gift of Dr. and Mrs. Sherman E. Lee in memory of Milton S. Fox. 71.166

Adoration of the Shepherds. Oil on panel, 16th c. Circle of Albrecht Dürer, German. H. 58. Holden Collection. 16.807

Virgin and Child in a Landscape. Oil on panel, 1531. Jan Gossaert (called Mabuse), Netherlandish. H. 48.9. John L. Severance Fund. 72.47

Portrait of Machtelt Suijs. Oil on panel, 1540s. Maerten van Heemskerck, Netherlandish. H. 74. Leonard C. Hanna, Jr., Fund. 87.136

Plaque: Portrait of Georg Knauer. Pearwood, dated 1537. Peter Dell, South German. H. 14. Purchase from the J. H. Wade Fund. 27.427

Portrait Medallion. Boxwood. Attr. to Friedrich Hagenauer, German, act. 1525-46. D. 7.3. Dudley P. Allen Fund. 27.421

A Stag Hunt. Oil on panel, 1540. Lucas Cranach the Elder, German. W. 170.2. John L. Severance Fund. 58.425

The Apocalypse: The Woman Clothed with the Sun. Engraving, 1546-56 (published 1561). Jean Duvet, French. H. 29.5. Gift of the Hanna Fund. 53.231

Portrait of Maria Kitscher von Oelkofen. Oil on panel, 1545. Hans Mielich, German. H. 64.1. The Elisabeth Severance Prentiss Collection. 44.88

Medal: The Trinity. Silver, signed: *H.R.,* dated 1544. Hans Reinhart the Elder, German, d. 1581. D. 10.2. Gift of G. Garretson Wade. 56.337

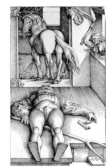

The Bewitched Groom. Woodcut, ca. 1544, before state I. H. 33.8. Hans Baldung (called Grien), German. Mr. and Mrs. Charles G. Prasse Collection 66.172

Plaquette: Venus and Cupid. Lead. Peter Flötner, German, act. Nuremberg, ca. 1485-1546. L. 9.2. Purchase from the J. H. Wade Fund. 84.15

The Dead Christ with Joseph of Arimathea. Oil on panel, ca. 1527. Giovanni Girolamo Savoldo, Italian. W. 191.8. Gift of the Hanna Fund. 52.512

Portrait of a Man. Oil on canvas, ca. 1525. Lorenzo Lotto, Italian, Venice. H. 109. Gift of the Hanna Fund. 50.250

Miniature: The Nativity. Tempera and gold on parchment. Girolamo dei Libri, Italian, Verona, 1474-1535. H. 16.4. Purchase from the J. H. Wade Fund. 53.281

Madonna and Child. Metalpoint on salmon prepared paper, ca. 1500-10. Lorenzo di Credi, Italian. H. 14.5. John L. Severance Fund. 63.472

Arrow Vase with Persian Inscriptions. Porcelain with underglaze blue decoration. Ming dynasty, Zhengde mark and period, 1506-21. H. 26.1. Millikin Collection.* 64.170

Study for the Sistine Chapel Ceiling (recto). Red chalk over black chalk, ca. 1511. Michelangelo Buonarroti. H. 34.3. Gift in memory of Henry G. Dalton by his nephews.* 40.465

Diogenes. After Parmigianino. Chiaroscuro woodcut, ca. 1524-27. Ugo da Carpi, Italian. H. 47.5. The Charles W. Harkness Endowment Fund. 23.1052

The Entombment. Etching, 1529-30. Parmigianino, Italian. H. 27.1. Dorothea Wright Hamilton Fund. 85.10

The Nativity. Pen and brown ink, brown wash heightened with white, ca. 1525-30. Parmigianino, Italian. H. 8.5. Dudley P. Allen Fund. 24.1003

The Healing of a Demoniac Woman. Red chalk, red wash, ca. 1557. Taddeo Zuccaro, Italian. H. 29. Gift of Robert Hays Gries. 39.662

Baluster Vase with Plum Blossoms: Fahua Ware. Stoneware with molded and modeled decoration. China, Ming dynasty, 16th c. H. 49.5. The Elisabeth Severance Prentiss Collection. 44.223

Fame. After Rosso Fiorentino. Engraving, ca. 1540, state I/II. Domenico del Barbiere, Italian. H. 28.7. Dudley P. Allen Fund. 88.106

The Wrath of Neptune. Bronze, ca. 1540. Attr. to Tiziano Minio, Italian, Padua-Venice. H. 36.1. Gift of Barrie Morrison. 74.273

Hat Jewel: The Rape of Helen. Enamel on gold. France, ca. 1560. D. 5.1. Purchase from the J. H. Wade Fund. 49.377

Portrait of a Married Couple. Oil on canvas, ca. 1550. Netherlandish Master. W. 141. Holden Collection. 16.793

Listening to the Bamboo. Hanging scroll, ink on paper. Wen Zhengming, Chinese, 1470-1559, Ming dynasty. H. 94.5. Leonard C. Hanna, Jr., Fund. 77.172

Candlesticks: Triumph of Diana and Labors of Hercules. Painted enamel on copper. Attr. to Jean Court, French, Limoges, act. 1555-65. H. 33.6. Purchase from the J. H. Wade Fund. 73.169.-.170

River Landscape in the Mountains. Etching, 1546. Augustin Hirschvogel, German. W. 17.5. John L. Severance Fund. 63.471

Cassone. Walnut. Italy, Venice, mid 16th c. L. 174.7. Bequest of John L. Severance. 42.607

Paschal Candlestick. Bronze. Attr. to Desiderio da Firenze, Italian, Padua, act. 1532-45. H. 123.2. Bequest of John L. Severance. 42.802

Mortar. Bronze, ca. 1550-60. Workshop of Wenzel Jamnitzer, German, Nuremberg. H. 11.8. Purchase from the J. H. Wade Fund. 51.444

Horse. Bronze, ca. 1560-70. After Gregor Erhart, German. H. 15.2. John L. Severance Fund. 52.108

Doorknocker with Gorgon Head and Emblem of the Cicogna Family. Bronze. Italy, Venice, mid 16th c. H. 25.4. Purchase from the J. H. Wade Fund. 72.1

Plate. Maiolica. Atelier of the Fontana family, Italy, Urbino, ca. 1560. D. 43.7. Bequest of John L. Severance. 42.622

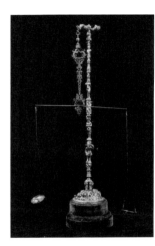

Two Funerary Figures. Hawthorn wood painted black, ca. 1570. Attr. to Germain Pilon, French. H. 62.2 and 61.3. John L. Severance Fund. 59.345-.346

Scales. Gilt bronze and silver, ca. 1565-70. Workshop of Wenzel Jamnitzer, German, Nuremberg, H. 37.5. Purchase from the J. H. Wade Fund. 50.382

Venus. Bronze, ca. 1560. Danese Cattaneo, Italian. H. 52.9. John L. Severance Fund. 50.578

Allegory of Life. Engraving, 1561, state IIa/VI. Giorgio Ghisi, Italian. W. 54.6. Leonard C. Hanna, Jr., Fund. 85.37

River and Mountains on a Clear Autumn Day. Handscroll, ink on paper. Dong Qichang, Chinese, 1555-1636, Ming dynasty. W. 136.8. Purchase from the J. H. Wade Fund. 59.46

Textile. Velvet weave; silk and gold. Iran, Safavid period, reign of Shah Tahmasp, 1524-76. H. 77.5. Purchase from the J. H. Wade Fund. 44.239

Akrura Drives Krishna and Balarama to Mathura. From *Isarda Bhagavata Purana.* Color on paper. India, prob. Delhi/Agra, ca. 1560-70. W. 25.7. John L. Severance Fund. 71.234

Daoist Retreat in Mountain and Stream. Hanging scroll, ink on paper, dated 1567. Lu Zhi, Chinese, Ming dynasty. H. 109.1. Purchase from the J. H. Wade Fund. 62.43

Carpet. Senna knot; wool and cotton. Iran, Herat, Safavid period, 16th c. H. 863.5. Florence and Charles Abel Oriental Rug Collection. 62.263

Poet-Musician. Fol. 110v of *Tuti-nama.* Color and gold on paper. India, Mughal school, reign of Akbar, ca. 1560. H. 20.3. Gift of Mrs. A. Dean Perry. 62.279

Alam Shah Closing the Dam at Shishan Pass. From *Dastan-i-Amir Hamza.* Color and gold on cotton. India, Mughal school, ca. 1570. H. 64.8. Gift of George P. Bickford. 76.74

The Qingbian Mountains. Hanging scroll, ink on paper. Dong Qichang, Chinese, 1555-1636, Ming dynasty. H. 224.5. Leonard C. Hanna, Jr., Fund. 80.10

Morning Sun Over the "Heavenly Citadel." Hanging scroll, ink and color on paper, dated 1614. Ding Yunpeng, Chinese, Ming dynasty. H. 212.7. Andrew R. and Martha Holden Jennings Fund. 65.28

Textile. Velvet weave; silk, gold, and silver. Iran, Safavid period, reign of Shah Tahmasp, 1524-76. H. 70. Purchase from the J. H. Wade Fund. 48.205

Chest. Oak. France, Normandy, 2d half 16th c. W. 175.3. Bequest of John L. Severance. 42.604

Seated Woman with Two Children. Alabaster. Attr. to Germain Pilon, French, ca. 1535-90. H. 29.8. Gift of Baroness R. de Kerchove. 51.541

Beaker with Figure of St. Mauritius. Enameled glass, dated 1568. Germany. H. 26. Gift of Mrs. Henry White Cannon. 48.232

Tigerware Jug with Silver-Gilt Mounts. Stoneware: Germany, Rhineland. Mounts: England, London, 1594-95. H. 23.8. Gift of Robert Hays Gries. 64.374

Adoration of the Magi. Oil on canvas, 1570s. Titian (Tiziano Vecelli), Italian, Venice. W. 228.3. Mr. and Mrs. William H. Marlatt Fund. 57.150

Ewer. White paste earthenware. France, St.-Porchaire, 16th c. H. 35.6. Purchase from the J. H. Wade Fund. 53.363

Jug with Arms of Cleves-Berg. Stoneware, dated 1580. Germany, Rhenish, Siegburg. H. 23.8. Andrew R. and Martha Holden Jennings Fund. 74.41

Virgin and Child Enthroned. Verre eglomisé. Italy, 2d half 16th c. Frame: silver and enamel. Germany, Augsburg, ca. 1600. H. 18.8. Purchase from the J. H. Wade Fund. 43.284

Portrait of a Woman. Oil on panel, mid 16th c. Agnolo Bronzino, Italian, Florence. H. 60. Leonard C. Hanna, Jr., Fund. 72.121

Portrait of Vincenzo Guarignoni. Oil on canvas, 1572. Giovanni Battista Moroni, Italian. H. 63. Gift of Adele C. and Howard P. Eells, Jr., in memory of Howard Parmelee Eells. 62.1

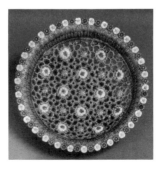

Mirror. Enamel "en resille." France, 2d half 16th c. H. 8.9. Purchase from the J. H. Wade Fund. 26.246

Plate with Openwork. Earthenware with lead glazes. Circle of Bernard Palissy, French, 16th c. D. 26. Purchase from the J. H. Wade Fund. 86.56

Standing Cup with Cover. Silver gilt. Germany, Nuremberg, 2d half 16th c. H. 49.5. John L. Severance Fund. 62.286

Baptism of Christ. Oil on canvas, ca. 1570. Tintoretto (Jacopo Robusti), Italian, Venice. W. 251.4. Gift of the Hanna Fund. 50.400

Lazarus and the Rich Man. Oil on canvas, ca. 1550. Jacopo Bassano, Italian. W. 221. Delia E. and L. E. Holden Funds. 39.68

Textile. Velvet weave; silk. Iran, Safavid period, reign of Shah Tahmasp, 1524-76. H. 31 (as mounted). Purchase from the J. H. Wade Fund. 44.499- 500

Female Daoist Figure in Landscape. Hanging scroll, ink on paper. Koboku, Japanese, act. 1st half 16th c., Muromachi period. H. 44.5. Leonard C. Hanna, Jr., Fund. 88.18

Portrait of Agostino Barbarigo. Oil on canvas, ca. 1571. Paolo Veronese, Italian. W. 104.2. Gift of Mrs. L. E. Holden, Mr. and Mrs. Guerdon S. Holden, and the L. E. Holden Fund. 28.16

Nushirwan and the Owls. From *Khamsa of Nizami.* Opaque watercolor, black and gold ink on paper. Iran, Safavid period, 16th c. H. 20.3. Purchase from the J. H. Wade Fund. 44.487

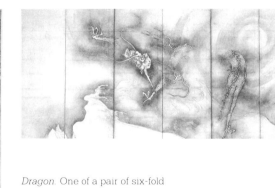

Dragon. One of a pair of six-fold screens, ink on paper. Sesson Shukei, Japanese, ca. 1504- ca. 1589, Muromachi period. W. 339. Purchase from the J. H. Wade Fund. 59.136

Plants above an Eroded Bank. Black chalk, brown and gray washes, and pink and white gouache, ca. 1565-70. Federico Barocci, Italian. H. 20. Purchase from the J. H. Wade Fund. 73.171

A Picnic in the Mountains. Ink drawing with opaque watercolor on paper. Iran, Tabriz, Safavid period, ca. 1550. H. 28.6. Purchase from the J. H. Wade Fund. 44.491

An Episode from the Story of Khusraw and Shirin. From *Khamsa of Nizami.* Opaque watercolor on paper. Iran, Safavid period, 16th c. H. 21.6. Purchase from the J. H. Wade Fund. 47.500

Half-Armor. Steel and niello. North Italy, 3d quarter 16th c. H. 26. Gift of Mr. and Mrs. John L. Severance. 16.1816

Camel with Attendant. Ink drawing with wash on paper, ca. 1545. Attr. to Sultan Muhammad, Iranian, Safavid period. W. 28.4. Purchase from the J. H. Wade Fund. 44.489

Large Dish: Bizen Ware. Stoneware. Japan, Momoyama period, late 16th c. D. 45.4. John L. Severance Fund. 83.8

Sir Anthony Mildmay.
Watercolor on vellum. Nicholas
Hilliard, English, ca. 1547-1619.
H. 23.5. Purchase from the J. H.
Wade Fund. 26.554

*Stained Glass Roundel: Arms of
the Canton of Zurich.* Workshop
of Hans Rütter, Swiss, act. late
16th c. D. 45.1. Purchase from
the J. H. Wade Fund. 55.71

The Judgment of Paris. Oil on
copper, 1602. Joachim Wtewael,
Dutch. W. 20.8. Mr. and Mrs.
William H. Marlatt Fund. 84.14

*Landscape with Venus and
Adonis.* Oil on copper, ca. 1600.
Gillis van Coninxloo, Netherlan-
dish. W. 53.6. Mr. and Mrs.
William H. Marlatt Fund. 62.293

Hercules and the Hydra. Bronze.
Attr. to Adriaen de Vries,
Netherlandish, ca. 1560-1626.
H. 46.7. Purchase from the J. H.
Wade Fund. 73.167

*Sextus Tarquinius Threatening
Lucrece.* Bronze, ca. 1600.
Hubert Gerhard, act. Germany.
H. 52.7. Purchase from the
J. H. Wade Fund. 62.245

Medici Plate. Soft paste porcelain. Italy, Florence, ca. 1580. D. 28. John L. Severance Fund. 49.489

John the Baptist. Bronze. Angelo de' Rossi, Italian, Verona, act. late 16th c. H. 49.5. John L. Severance Fund. 52.276

Youth Sleeping under a Willow Tree. Opaque watercolor and gold on paper, ca. 1590. Attr. to Aga Riza, Iran, Safavid period. H. 21.5. Purchase from the J. H. Wade Fund. 44.494

Humuyan's Victory over the Afghans. From the *Akbar Nama.* Color on paper. India, Mughal school, ca. 1590. H. 31.1. Andrew R. and Martha Holden Jennings Fund. 71.77

The Five Hundred Arhats (detail). Handscroll, ink and color on paper. Wu Bin, Chinese, act. ca. 1567-ca. 1617, Ming dynasty. Overall W. 2345.2. John L. Severance Fund. 71.16

Angel. Wax (model for a figure crowning pediment, Church of Santa Maria presso San Celso). Annibale Fontana, Italian, Milan, ca. 1583/4. H. 54. Leonard C. Hanna, Jr., Fund. 84.38

Mars. Bronze, ca. 1587. Giambologna, Italian. H. 39. Purchase from the J. H. Wade Fund. 64.421

Rustam's Guide Owland Tied to a Tree. From *Shahnama of Shah Abbas.* Opaque watercolor on paper, signed, 4th quarter 16th c. Sadiqi Bek, Iran. H. 23.5. Andrew R. and Martha Holden Jennings Fund. 88.101

Greeting the Spring (detail). Handscroll, ink and color on paper, dated 1600. Wu Bin, Chinese, Ming dynasty. Overall W. 245.1. Purchase from the J. H. Wade Fund. 59.45

Box with Pierced Cover. Porcelain with five-color overglaze enamel decoration. China, Ming dynasty, Wanli mark and period, 1573-1619. L. 25.2. John L. Severance Fund. 66.117

The Feast of the Gods. Bronze, ca. 1575. Alessandro Vittoria, Italian, Venice. H. 34.4. John L. Severance Fund. 52.464

Study for "Aeneas' Flight from Troy." Pen and brown ink, brown wash, opaque water-color, over black chalk, ca. 1587/8. Federico Barocci,

Italian. W. 42.6. L. E. Holden Fund. 60.26

Dragon in Foliage. Ink drawing on paper with opaque water-color and gold in corners. Turkey, Istanbul, Ottoman period, mid 16th c. W. 40.2.

Purchase from the J. H. Wade Fund. 44.492

Seven Deities: Nox. Chiaroscuro woodcut printed in black and gray, 1588-90. Hendrik Goltzius, Dutch. H. 34.6. Andrew R. and Martha Holden Jennings Fund. 90.86

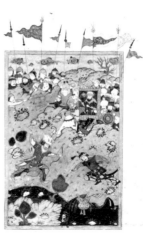

Lamentation over the Body of Christ. Woodcut. Giuseppe Scolari, Italian, act. 1592-1607. H. 44.4. Gift of The Print Club of Cleveland. 82.170

Landscape with a Boat. Pen and brown ink, ca. 1590. Annibale Carracci, Italian. W. 40.5. Purchase from the J. H. Wade Fund. 72.101

Rustam Meets the Challenge of Ashkabus. From *Shanama of Firdawsi.* Opaque watercolor and gold on paper. Turkey, Provincial school, ca. 1590-1600. H. 25.4. Gift of John C. Heege. 60.199

Bottle-Vase with Fish Design: Punch'ong Ware. Glazed stoneware with incised decoration. Korea, Choson period, 16th c. H. 30.5. John L. Severance Fund. 62.153

Boating in Moonlight. Album leaf, ink and color on silk. Korea, Choson period, 16th c. H. 30. John L. Severance Fund. 89.87

Water Jar (Mizusashi). Shino ware, glazed stoneware. Japan, Momoyama period, 16th c. H. 18.4. John L. Severance Fund. 72.9

Phoenix and Paulownia. One of a pair of six-fold screens, ink,color, and gold on paper. Attr. to Tosa Mitsuyoshi, Japanese, 1539-1613, Momoyama period. W. 362.

Leonard C. Hanna, Jr., Fund. 86.2

Disasters. Leaf from *Tairikh-i-Alfi (History of a Thousand Years).* Color on paper. India, Mughal school, ca. 1595. H. 42.3. Dudley P. Allen Fund. 32.36

Landscape with Figures. Hanging scroll, ink on silk, dated 1584. Kim Che, Korean, Choson period. W. 67.2. Mr. and Mrs. William H. Marlatt Fund. 87.187

Cosmetic Box with Wisteria Design. Lacquer on wood. Japan, Momoyama period, 1573-1615. W. 33.3. Andrew R. and Martha Holden Jennings Fund. 66.25

Pampas Grasses. One of a pair of six-fold screens, ink, color, and gold on paper. Japan, Momoyama period, 1573-1615. W. 348.8. John L. Severance Fund. 84.43

Siege of Arbela. From *Chingiz Nama.* Color and gold on paper, ca. 1596. Basawan and Sur Das Gujerati, Indian, Mughal school. H. 38.7. Purchase from the J. H. Wade Fund. 47.502

1539-1615

The Holy Family with Mary Magdalene. Oil on canvas, 1500s. El Greco, Spanish. H. 130. Gift of Friends of The Cleveland Museum of Art, in memory of J. H. Wade. 26.247

The Virgin with a Spindle. Etching and engraving, ca. 1611-13, state II/III. Jacques Bellange, French. H. 25.1. Gift of The Print Club of Cleveland in honor of Louise S. Richards. 86.244

Still Life. Oil on copper, 1606. Ambrosius Bosschaert the Elder, Dutch. H. 35.6. Gift of Carrie Moss Halle in memory of Salmon Portland Halle. 60.108

The Crucifixion of St. Andrew. Oil on canvas, ca. 1607. Michelangelo Merisi da Caravaggio, Italian. H. 202.5. Leonard C. Hanna, Jr., Fund. 76.2

Christ on the Cross with Landscape. Oil on canvas, ca. 1605. El Greco, Spanish. H. 193. Gift of the Hanna Fund. 52.222

Diana and Her Nymphs Departing for the Chase. Oil on canvas, ca. 1615. Peter Paul Rubens, Flemish. H. 215.9. Leonard C. Hanna, Jr., Fund. 59.190

The Mocking of Ceres. After Adam Elsheimer. Engraving, 1610. Hendrik Goudt, Dutch. H. 32. Mr. and Mrs. Lewis B. Williams Collection by exchange. 81.23

Venus and Cupid. Pen and brown ink, brown wash, over red chalk indications, ca. 1615. Guercino (Giovanni Francesco Barbieri), Italian. W. 39.4. Dudley P. Allen Fund. 25.1188

Portrait of Isabella Brant. Oil on panel, ca. 1622. Peter Paul Rubens, Flemish. H. 55.8. Mr. and Mrs. William H. Marlatt Fund. 47.207

The Idolatry of Solomon. Black chalk, pen and brown ink, brown wash heightened with white, ca. 1620-22. Pietro da Cortona, Italian. W. 44.2. John L. Severance Fund. 87.142

Iran   India   Japan

89

1558–1640

Carpet. Senna knot; silk and cotton. Iran, Isfahan, Safavid period, ca. 1600. H. 206.5. Purchase from the J. H. Wade Fund. 26.533

Jain Ascetic Walking along a Riverbank. Color on paper. Basawan, Indian, Mughal school, ca. 1600. H. 38.9. Gift of Severance and Greta Millikin. 67.244

Antelope and Deer Hunt. Color on paper, ca. 1607-08. Govardhan, Indian, Mughal school. H. 37.2. Dudley P. Allen Fund. 39.66

Bowl with Christian Design of Cross and Insignia of the Society of Jesus: Hagi Ware. Glazed stoneware with inlaid design. Japan, Momoyama period, ca. 1600. D. 31. John L. Severance Fund. 62.211

Poem Card (Shikishi). Card mounted on a hanging scroll, gold, silver, and ink on paper, dated 1606. Hon'ami Koetsu and Tawaraya Sotatsu, Japanese, Momoyama-Edo period.

H. 20. John L. Severance Fund. 87.60

Courtly Procession. Opaque watercolor on paper. Iran, Safavid period, ca. 1600. H. 43.8. Purchase from the J. H. Wade Fund. 62.24

Vabhruvahana Approaches Arjuna. From a *Razm Nama (Book of Wars).* Color on paper, ca. 1610-17. India, Mughal school. H. 35.5. Mr. and Mrs. William H. Marlatt Fund. 60.44

Imperial Rooster. Color on paper, signed: Dilaram Pandit Kashmiri. Indian, Mughal school, ca. 1620. H. 18.3. Gift of Herbert F. Leisy. 44.501

Dish with Design of Valerian and Rocks in a Garden: Nezumi Shino Ware. Glazed stoneware. Japan, Momoyama period, ca. 1610. W. 23.4. John L. Severance Fund. 66.24

Noh Robe. Silk embroidery on silk ground with (beaten) gold leaf. Japan, early 17th c. L. 158.5. John L. Severance Fund. 74.36

Youth with Toy. Opaque watercolor and gold on paper. Iran, Safavid period, early 17th c. H. 26.7. Purchase from the J. H. Wade Fund. 47.497

Prince and Ascetics. Color on paper. Attr. to Govardhan, India, Mughal school, reign of Shah Jahan, ca. 1630. H. 37.5. Andrew R. and Martha Holden Jennings Fund. 71.79

The Beach at Sumiyoshi, from *Ise Monogatari (Tales of Ise).* Album leaf, color and gold on paper. Tawaraya Sotatsu, Japanese, act. ca. 1600-40, Edo period. H. 24.5. John L. Severance Fund. 51.398

Poem Scroll (detail). Handscroll, ink and color on silk. Hon'ami Koetsu, 1558-1637 (calligraphy), and Tawaraya Sotatsu, act. ca. 1600-40 (painting), Japanese, Momoyama-Edo period.

Overall L. 543.4. Leonard C. Hanna, Jr., Fund. 72.67

Still Life with Sweets. Oil on canvas, 1622. Juan van der Hamen, Spanish. W. 97. John L. Severance Fund. 80.6

The Repentant Magdalene. Oil on canvas, ca. 1630. Simon Vouet, French. H. 130.8. Leonard C. Hanna, Jr., Fund. 88.108

A Genoese Woman with Her Child. Oil on canvas, ca. 1623-25. Anthony van Dyck, Flemish. H. 217.8. Gift of the Hanna Fund. 54.392

Samson and Delilah. Oil on canvas, ca. 1620. Gerrit van Honthorst, Dutch. H. 129. Mr. and Mrs. William H. Marlatt Fund. 68.23

The Holy House of Nazareth. Oil on canvas, ca. 1630. Francisco de Zurbarán, Spanish. W. 220.2. Leonard C. Hanna, Jr., Fund. 60.117

Samson. Oil on canvas, 1631. Valentin de Boulogne, French. H. 135.6. Mr. and Mrs. William H. Marlatt Fund. 72.50

The Feast of Herod (recto). Black and red chalk, pen and brown ink, ca. 1638. Peter Paul Rubens, Flemish. W. 47.3. Delia E. Holden and L. E. Holden Funds. 54.2

Heraclitus. Oil on canvas, 1621. Hendrik ter Brugghen, Dutch. H. 125. Mr. and Mrs. William H. Marlatt Fund. 77.2

Portrait of the Jester Calabazas. Oil on canvas, ca. 1632. Diego Velázquez, Spanish. H. 175. Leonard C. Hanna, Jr., Fund. 65.15

The Bear Hunt. Oil on panel, 1639. Peter Paul Rubens, Flemish. W. 53.7. Leonard C. Hanna, Jr., Fund. 83.69

Kast. Oak with ebony and rosewood veneers. Holland, 2d quarter 17th c. H. 244.5. Purchase from the J. H. Wade Fund. 82.57

Flute Glass. Engraved glass. Germany, Thuringia, early 17th c. H. 33. John L. Severance Fund. 51.545

Double Pokal. Silver gilt, ca. 1614-32. Alexander Treghart, German, Nuremberg. H. 58. Purchase from the J. H. Wade Fund. 70.108-.109

Danae. Oil on canvas, ca. 1621. Orazio Gentileschi, Italian. W. 228.6. Leonard C. Hanna, Jr., Fund. 71.101

Namban Byobu: Screen of the Southern Barbarians. One of a pair of six-fold screens, ink, color, and gold on paper. Japan, Momoyama period, ca. 1610-64. W. 334.3. Leonard C. Hanna, Jr., Fund. 60.194

Amor. Oil on canvas, 1620s. Johann Liss, German. H. 87.7. Leonard C. Hanna, Jr., Fund. 71.100

Head of Proserpina. Terracotta, ca. 1621-22. Giovanni Lorenzo Bernini, Italian, Rome. H. 13.5. John L. Severance Fund. 68.101

Rest on the Flight into Egypt. Oil on canvas, 1624. Guercino (Giovanni Francesco Barbieri), Italian. D. 68.5. Mr. and Mrs. William H. Marlatt Fund. 67.123

Rape of the Sabines. Oil on canvas, ca. 1640-42. Johann Heinrich Schönfeld, German. W. 160. Leonard C. Hanna, Jr., Fund. 82.143

Portrait of a Man. Oil on canvas, ca. 1628. Antonio Tanzio da Varallo, Italian. H. 97.8. Leonard C. Hanna, Jr., Fund. 85.143

Spain	France	Holland

The Death of Adonis. Oil on canvas, ca. 1650. Italian follower of Jusepe de Ribera. W. 238.8. Mr. and Mrs. William H. Marlatt Fund. 65.19

Nymphs and Satyrs or *Amor Vincit Omnia.* Oil on canvas, ca. 1625. Nicolas Poussin, French. W. 127.5. Gift of J. H. Wade. 26.26

Enclosed Valley. Etching on linen, colored by hand, ca. 1623-30, state I/IV,b. Hercules Segers, Dutch. W. 19. John L. Severance Fund. 51.349

St. Jerome. Oil on canvas, ca. 1640-50. Jusepe de Ribera, Spanish. H. 129. Mr. and Mrs. William H. Marlatt Fund. 61.219

Landscape. Oil on canvas, 1630s. Claude Gellée (called Lorrain), French. W. 137. Mr. and Mrs. William H. Marlatt Fund. 46.73

Portrait of a Youth. Oil on panel, 1632. Isaak de Joudreville, Dutch. H. 57.8. Bequest of John L. Severance. 42.644

Portrait of a Woman. Oil on panel, 1635. Rembrandt van Rijn, Dutch. H. 77.5. The Elisabeth Severance Prentiss Collection. 44.90

Landscape with Hunters. Oil on canvas, ca. 1635. Gaspard Dughet, French. W. 175.2. John L. Severance Fund. 70.30

Hunting Party Near Ruins. Oil on canvas, 1646. Jan Baptist Weenix, Dutch. W. 129.2. Severance and Greta Millikin Collection. 64.294

Journey of a Patriarch. Oil on canvas, ca. 1640. Giovanni Benedetto Castiglione, Italian. W. 78.4. Mr. and Mrs. William H. Marlatt Fund. 69.1

Adoration of the Magi. Oil on canvas, 1642. Guido Reni, Italian. H. 367.3. Leonard C. Hanna, Jr., Fund. 69.132

A Young, Angry Heroine. From Bhanu Datta's *Rasamanjari.* Color on paper. India, Rajasthan, Mewar school, ca. 1615-20. H. 25.4. Mr. and Mrs. William H. Marlatt Fund. 60.52

Sakyamuni Under the Bodhi Tree. Hanging scroll, ink and color on silk. China, Ming dynasty, early 17th c. H. 129. Purchase from the J. H. Wade Fund. 71.68

Portrait of a Woman. Oil on canvas, 1638. Frans Hals, Dutch. H. 69.7. Purchase from the J. H. Wade Fund. 48.137

Minerva. Black and red chalk, ca. 1640. Bernardo Strozzi, Italian. H. 37.2. John L. Severance Fund. 53.626

Minerva. Oil on canvas, ca. 1640. Bernardo Strozzi, Italian. H. 147.3. Gift of Friends of The Cleveland Museum of Art. 29.133

St. Catherine of Siena Receiving the Crown of Thorns and a Rosary from the Christ Child. Oil on canvas, ca. 1643. Sassoferrato (Giovanni Battista Salvi), Italian. W. 84. Mr. and Mrs. William H. Marlatt Fund. 66.332

Krishna. From the *Rasikapriya.* Color on paper, dated 1634. India, Rajasthan, Malwa school. H. 20.8. Gift of Nasli M. Heeramaneck. 38.303

Adoration of the Shepherds. Oil on canvas, ca. 1645-50. Bernardo Cavallino, Italian, Naples. W. 148.3. Mr. and Mrs. William H. Marlatt Fund. 68.100

Xuan-wen Jun Giving Instructions on the Classics. Hanging scroll, ink and color on silk, dated 1638. Chen Hongshou, Chinese, Ming dynasty. H. 173.7. Mr. and Mrs. William H. Marlatt Fund. 61.89

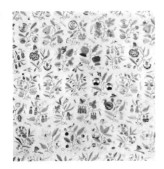

Embroidered Panel. Tabby linen ground; polychrome silk. England, James I period, early 17th c. H. 66. Purchase from the J. H. Wade Fund. 33.421

The Repentant St. Peter. Oil on canvas, 1645. Georges de La Tour, French. H. 114. Gift of the Hanna Fund. 51.454

The Tree of Christ. Black chalk, touches of pen and brown ink, over graphite, 1635-40. Laurent de La Hyre, French. W. 46.4. Delia E. Holden Fund. 72.98

View of Emmerich. Oil on panel, 1645. Jan van Goyen, Dutch. W. 95.3. John L. Severance Fund. 59.351

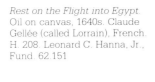

Panel (detail): *King Henry VIII Treading on the Pope.* Petit point embroidery; silk. England, reign of Charles I, 1625-49. Overall W. 55.3. Gift of J. H. Wade. 19.585

Study for Extreme Unction (recto). Pen and brown ink, brown wash, 1643/4. Nicolas Poussin, French. W. 22. Leonard C. Hanna, Jr., Fund. 83.197

Wooded Landscape with Sleeping Peasants (Parable of the Tares of the Field). Oil on canvas, 1650-53. Simon de Vlieger, Dutch. W. 130.4. Mr. and Mrs. William H. Marlatt Fund. 75.76

Rest on the Flight into Egypt. Oil on canvas, 1640s. Claude Gellée (called Lorrain), French. H. 208. Leonard C. Hanna, Jr., Fund. 62.151

The Holy Family on the Steps. Oil on canvas, 1648. Nicolas Poussin, French. W. 111.7. Leonard C. Hanna, Jr., Fund. 81.18

Landscape with a Cottage and Figures. Black chalk, gray wash, 1655. Jan van Goyen, Dutch. W. 27.5. Dudley P. Allen Fund. 29.548

Witch Scenes. Two of four tondi. Oil on canvas, ca. 1645. Salvator Rosa, Italian. D. 54.5. Purchase from the J. H. Wade Fund. 77.39-40

Small Black and White Bird on a Shrub with Butterflies. Opaque watercolor on paper. Shafi 'Abbasi, Iranian, Isfahan, mid 17th c.(?) L. 24.9. Andrew R. and Martha Holden Jennings Fund. 71.84

Guanyin: Dehua Ware. Glazed porcelain. China, Ming dynasty, 17th c. H. 45.1. The Norweb Collection. 50.579

Deposition from the Cross. Ivory, 1653. Adam Lenckhardt, Austrian. H. 44.8. John L. Severance Fund. 67.134

The Standard Bearer. Mezzotint, 1658, state I/III. Prince Rupert von der Pfalz, German. H. 28.3. Dudley P. Allen Fund. 66.10

Adoration of the Shepherds. Oil on canvas, ca. 1640. Carlo Dolci, Italian. H. 88.6. Mr. and Mrs. William H. Marlatt Fund. 68.22

Baptism of Christ. Bronze, ca. 1650-54. Alessandro Algardi, Italian, Rome. H. 62.5. Andrew R. and Martha Holden Jennings Fund. 65.471

Textile. Velvet weave; silk and gold. Iran, Safavid period, reign of Shah Abbas, 1587-1628. H. 157.5. Purchase from the J. H. Wade Fund. 32.42

Zheng Yang Xu Moving His Family. Hanging scroll, ink and color on silk. Cui Zizhong, Chinese, act. ca. 1594-1644, Ming dynasty. H. 165.6. Mr. and Mrs. William H. Marlatt Fund. 61.90

The Vision of St. Jerome. Oil on canvas, ca. 1660s. Giovanni Battista Langetti, Italian. H. 200.2. Delia E. and L. E. Holden Funds. 51.334

Pope Innocent X. Bronze, 2d half 17th c. Alessandro Algardi, Italian, Rome. H. 78.1. Gift of Rosenberg & Stiebel, Inc.* 57.496

Textile (detail). Lampas weave, brocaded; silk, gold, and silver. Iran, Safavid period, 17th c. Overall H. 88.2. Purchase from the J. H. Wade Fund. 53.17

England	France	Flanders	Holland

Portrait of Mrs. Leneve. Oil on canvas, ca. 1658. Peter Lely, English. H. 126.7. Gift of Mrs. Otto Miller. 42.247

Dance of Boys and Girls. Oil on canvas. Le Nain Brothers, French, 17th c. W. 120.2. Gift of Mrs. Salmon P. Halle in Memory of Salmon Portland Halle. 57.489

Aeneas Takes Leave of Dido. Tapestry weave; silk and wool. Flanders, Antwerp, mid 17th c. H. 403.8. Gift of Mrs. Francis F. Prentiss, in memory of Dr. Dudley P. Allen. 15.85

Windmill near Fields. Oil on panel, 1646. Jacob van Ruisdael, Dutch. W. 68.5. Mr. and Mrs. William H. Marlatt Fund. 67.19

Story of David and Bathsheba. Stumpwork embroidery; silk, metallic yarns, pearls, carved wood on silk. England, dated 1658. W. 53.3. Bequest of Florence LaGanke Harris. 73.186

Pastoral Scene with Classical Figures. Pen and dark brown ink, brown and gray wash, over graphite, 1640-45. Claude Gellée (called Lorrain). W. 25.8. Leonard C. Hanna, Jr., Fund. 82.13

The Three Crosses. Etching, drypoint, and engraving, 1653-60, state IV/V. Rembrandt van Rijn, Dutch. W. 44.2. Bequest of Ralph King and Purchase from the J. H. Wade Fund. 59.241

Charles II, King of England. Oil on canvas, 1653. Philippe de Champaigne, French. H. 125.7. The Elisabeth Severance Prentiss Fund. 59.38

Landscape with a Dead Tree. Oil on canvas, 1660s. Jacob van Ruisdael, Dutch. W. 131. Mr. and Mrs. William H. Marlatt Fund. 67.63

Tobias Healing His Father's Blindness. Pen and brown ink, corrected with white gouache, ca. 1640-45. Rembrandt van Rijn, Dutch. H. 21.1. Purchase from the J. H. Wade Fund. 69.69

St. Jerome Reading in an Italian Landscape. Etching, engraving, and drypoint on oatmeal paper, ca. 1653, state II/II. Rembrandt van Rijn, Dutch. H. 25.8. Bequest of Mrs. Severance A. Millikin. 89.233

The Feast of Terminus. Red pigment, 1660-65. Giovanni Benedetto Castiglione, Italian. W. 56.3. Delia E. Holden Fund. 64.31

Portrait of Akbar. Grisaille. Attr. to Govardhan, India, Mughal school, ca. 1640-50. H. 25.4. Andrew R. and Martha Holden Jennings Fund. 71.78

Reclining Water Buffalo. Jade (nephrite). China, Ming dynasty, 1368-1644. L. 21. Gift of Mrs. John Lyon Collyer in memory of her mother, Mrs. G. M. G. Forman. 60.282

Descent from the Cross by Torchlight. Etching and drypoint, 1654. Rembrandt van Rijn, Dutch. H. 20.9. Leonard C. Hanna, Jr., Fund. 86.77

Portrait of a Man. Oil on canvas, ca. 1660. Attr. to Rembrandt van Rijn, Dutch. H. 84.5. Gift of the Hanna Fund. 50.252

The Approach of Krishna. From Bhanu Datta's *Rasamanjari.* Color on paper. India, Pahari, Basohli school, ca. 1660-70. H. 23.3. Edward L. Whittemore Fund. 65.249

Box with Cover. Lacquered wood with inset wickerwork. China, Ming dynasty, 17th c. W. 13.8. Edward L. Whittemore Fund. 65.30

The Meeting of Christ with Martha and Mary after the Death of Lazarus. Pen and brown ink, corrected with white, ca. 1662-65. Rembrandt van Rijn, Dutch. W. 20.8.

Leonard C. Hanna, Jr., Fund. 62.116

Siva and Parvati Seated on an Elephant Skin. Color on paper. India Pahari, Basohli school, ca. 1675-80. H. 23.2. Edward L. Whittemore Fund. 52.587

Hoop-Backed Armchair. Burmese or East Indian rosewood (*huang huali*) and woven reed. China, late Ming dynasty, 17th c. H. 85.4. The Norweb Collection. 55.40

Spoon. Silver, 1661. John Hull and Robert Sanderson, American, Boston. L. 15.9. Gift of Hollis French. 40.214

Covered Cup. Silver, 1677/8. I.A. (unidentified), English, London. H. 17.2. In honor of William Mathewson Milliken in appreciation of his interest in Cleveland artists. 58.422

The Kiss of Peace and Justice. Oil on canvas, 1654. Laurent de La Hyre, French. W. 76.2. John L. Severance Fund. 71.102

The Betrayal of Christ. Oil on canvas, 1650s. Jacob Jordaens, Flemish. W. 246.3. Leonard C. Hanna, Jr., Fund. 70.32

Covered Cup. Silver, 1686/7. W. I. (unidentified), English, London. H. 23.8. Inspired by the great benefits accomplished for humanity by Dr. George W. Crile, I give this James II cup to The Cleveland Museum of Art in his honor. Gift of Grace Studebaker Fish. 35.145

Blessed Alessandro Sauli. Terracotta, ca. 1663-68. Pierre Puget, French. H. 69.9. Andrew R. and Martha Holden Jennings Fund. 64.36

Head of a Philosopher. Marble, dated 1662. Pierre Puget, French. H. 39.7. Leonard C. Hanna, Jr., Fund. 69.121

The Conversion of St. Paul with Horseman and Banner. Black and red chalk, pen and gray ink, and colored washes, 1645-47. Jacob Jordaens, Flemish. H. 32.8. Delia E. Holden and L. E. Holden Funds. 54.366

Peasants with Cattle and Sheep in a Stream. Oil on canvas, ca. 1670. Jan Siberechts, Flemish. W. 122.5. Mr. and Mrs. William H. Marlatt Fund. 69.18

Seated Peasant Woman. Red chalk over black chalk indications, before 1671. Adriaen van de Velde, Dutch. W. 23.4. John L. Severance Fund. 66.239

Travelers in a Hilly Landscape. Oil on panel, ca. 1650. Aelbert Cuyp, Dutch. W. 74.8. Bequest of John L. Severance. 42.637

Flowers of Four Seasons. One of a pair of six-fold screens, ink and color on paper. Tawaraya Sosetsu, Japanese, act. mid 17th c., Edo period. W. 330.7. Leonard C. Hanna, Jr., Fund. 68.193

Still Life. Oil on canvas, 1663. Willem Kalf, Dutch. H. 60.3. Leonard C. Hanna, Jr., Fund. 62.292

Dune Landscape with Figures. Oil on panel, ca. 1650s. Philips Wouwermans, Dutch. W. 41.5. Mr. and Mrs. William H. Marlatt Fund. 67.124

Landscape in the Style of Dong Yuan and Juran. Hanging scroll, ink and white pigment on silk, dated 1650 in inscription of 1670. Gong Xian, Chinese, Qing dynasty. H. 216.3. Andrew R. and Martha Holden Jennings Fund. 69.123

The Four Accomplishments. Hanging scroll, ink, color, and gold on paper. Attr. to Iwasa Matabei, Japanese, 1578-1650, Edo period. H. 115.3. The Kelvin Smith Collection, given by Mrs. Kelvin Smith. 85.269

Portrait of a Woman Standing. Oil on canvas, ca. 1665. Gerard ter Borch, Dutch. H. 63.3. The Elisabeth Severance Prentiss Collection. 44.93

View of the Heerengracht, Amsterdam. Oil on canvas, ca. 1661. Jan Wijnants, Dutch. W. 81.9. Gift of Harry D. Kendrick. 64.419

Seasonal Landscapes. Album, ink and color on paper, dated 1668. Xiao Yuncong, Chinese, Qing dynasty. H. 21. John L. Severance Fund. 55.302

Laban Searching for His Stolen Household Gods in Rachel's Tent. Oil on canvas, ca. 1665. Bartolomé Murillo. W. 375. Gift of the John Huntington Art and Polytechnic Trust. 65.469

Ebony Cabinet. Wood, metal, and tortoise shell, ca. 1690. Attr. to André-Charles Boulle, French, Paris. H. 101.3. John L. Severance Fund. 49.539

A Rooster and a Turkey Fighting. Oil on canvas, late 17th c. Melchior de Hondecoeter, Dutch. W. 166.4. John L. Severance Fund. 86.59

The Assumption of the Virgin: Oil Sketch. On panel, 1670. Juan de Valdés Leal, Spanish. H. 40.3. Leonard C. Hanna, Jr., Fund. 87.7

Pair of Bed Hangings. Petit point embroidery; silk and wool. France, Paris, ca. 1690. H. 330.7. Purchase from the J. H. Wade Fund. 90.24-.25.

Virgin and Child. Pen and brown ink, brown wash, over red and black chalk, ca 1670. Bartolomé Murillo, Spanish. H. 21.4. Mr. and Mrs. Charles G. Prasse Collection. 68.66

Clock. Wood, metal, and tortoise shell, ca. 1695. André-Charles Boulle, French, Paris. H. 113.7. Gift in honor of Emery May Holden Norweb and Raymond Henry Norweb. 67.153

Interior of a Church. Oil on canvas, ca. 1680. Emanuel de Witte, Dutch. H. 62. Mr. and Mrs. William H. Marlatt Fund. 71.1

The Immaculate Conception. Oil on canvas, 1670s. Bartolomé Murillo, Spanish. H. 220.5. Leonard C. Hanna, Jr., Fund. 59.189

Vase. Soft paste porcelain. France, Rouen or Saint-Cloud, ca. 1700. H. 21.6. Purchase from the J. H. Wade Fund. 47.63

A Cottage in the Woods. Oil on canvas, ca. 1662. Meindert Hobbema, Dutch. W. 111.8. Bequest of John L. Severance. 42.641

Bust of a Man. Marble, ca. 1680. Circle of Ercole Ferrata, Italian. H. 81.5. The Thomas L. Fawick Memorial Collection. 79.39

Shri Raga. Color on paper. India, Rajasthan, Mewar school, ca. 1680. H. 38. Edward L. Whittemore Fund. 31.451

Evening Shower. Hanging scroll, ink on silk. Kano Tanyu, Japanese, 1602-74, Edo period, H. 144.5. Mr. and Mrs. William H. Marlatt Fund. 85.27

The Music Party. Oil on canvas, 1663. Pieter de Hooch, Dutch. W. 119.4. Gift of the Hanna Fund. 51.355

Famous Views of Lake Biwa. One of a pair of six-fold screens, ink, color, and gold on paper. Kano school, Japan, Edo period, mid 17th c. W. 344.5. Purchase from the J. H. Wade Fund. 83.20

Esther, Ahasuerus, and Haman. Oil on canvas, ca. 1665-69. Jan Steen, Dutch. W. 92.9. John L. Severance Fund. 64.153

Horse Race at Kamo Shrine. One of a pair of six-fold screens, ink, color, and gold on paper. Japan, Edo period, mid 17th c. W. 362. Purchase from the J. H. Wade Fund. 76.96

Mountainous Landscape. Black chalk, pen and black ink, black wash, 1679-80. Claes Berchem, Dutch. W. 52. Delia E. Holden Fund. 58.410

Chasuble: Sacred and Profane Love. Embroidery; silk and metallic threads on silk. Germany, last quarter 17th c. H. 116. John L. Severance Fund. 71.235

Covered Cup. Silver and silver gilt, 1688. Johann Andreas Thelot, German, Augsburg. H. 40. Purchase from the J. H. Wade Fund. 66.111.

Flounce. Lace, *gros point de Venise;* linen. Italy, Venice, 17th c. W. 118.7. Gift of John Sherwin, Jr., and Francis M. Sherwin in memory of their mother, Mrs. John Sherwin. 36.82

Still Life with Gooseberries. Oil on paper mounted on panel, 1701. Adriaen Coorte, Dutch. H. 29.5. Leonard C. Hanna, Jr., Fund. 87.32

Goblet. Engraved glass, 1680. Herman Schwinger, German, Nuremberg. H. 31.1. John L. Severance Fund. 50.389

Venus and Satyr with Cupid. Ivory, ca. 1690s. Ignaz Elhafen, German. H. 15.5. Andrew R. and Martha Holden Jennings Fund. 82.144

The Vision of St. Francis of Assisi. Oil on canvas, 1680s. Luca Giordano, Italian. H. 240. Mr. and Mrs. William H. Marlatt Fund. 66.125

Education of the Virgin. Marble, ca. 1694 or later. Attr. to Giuseppe Mazzuoli, Italian. H. 108.6. John L. Severance Fund. 73.6

Tankard. Silver, partially gilt. Andreas Brachfeldt, Latvian, Riga, late 17th c. *Relief.* Silver. Master D. M., German, Augsburg. H. 25.3. John L. Severance Fund. 71.266

Rest on the Flight into Egypt. Terracotta, ca. 1700-10. Giuseppe Maria Mazza, Italian. H. 32.2. John L. Severance Fund. 64.427

Head of a King. Bronze. Africa, Nigeria, Benin City, ca. 17th c. H. 29.9. Dudley P. Allen Fund. 38.6

Millefleur Carpet (detail). Senna knot; silk and wool. India, Mughal school, late 17th c. Overall H. 292.7. Dudley P. Allen Fund. 36.17

Hookah Bottle. Blue glass with gold. India, Mughal school, ca. 1700. H. 19.7. Cornelia Blakemore Warner Fund. 61.44

Plaque of a Warrior-Priest. Bronze. Africa, Nigeria, Benin City, ca. 17th c. H. 49.4. John L. Severance Fund. 53.425

Panels from a Box. Ivory. India, Mughal school, Northeast Deccan, ca. 1700. W. 30.3. Gift of George P. Bickford. 69.229

Storage Jar with Dragon Design. Porcelain with underglaze blue decoration. Korea, Choson period, 17th c. H. 39.4. Leonard C. Hanna, Jr., Fund. 86.85

Storage Jar with Dragon and Clouds. Stoneware with underglaze iron decoration. Korea, Choson period, 17th c. H. 35.5. Leonard C. Hanna, Jr., Fund. 86.69

Storage Jar. Glazed porcelain. Korea, Choson period, 17th c. H. 35.4. Purchase from the J. H. Wade Fund. 83.28

Portrait of a Korean Priest. Hanging scroll, ink, color and gold on silk. Korea, Choson period, 17th c. H. 114.7. Mr. and Mrs. William H. Marlatt Fund. 90.16

Mask of an Elder. Wood with lacquer and horsehair. Korea, Choson period, 17th-18th c. H. 20.3. The Severance and Greta Millikin Purchase Fund. 89.103

Tea Storage Jar: Shigaraki-type Ware. Glazed stoneware. Nonomura Ninsei, ca. 1645-80/90, Japanese, Edo period. H. 28.3. Purchase from the J. H. Wade Fund. 78.6

Prunus. Hanging scroll, ink on silk. Ogata Korin, Japanese, 1658-1716, Edo period. H. 97. John L. Severance Fund. 83.10

Plate with Pine, Prunus, and Bird: Kutani Ware. Porcelain with overglaze enamel decoration. Japan, Edo period, late 17th c. D. 37.5. Gift of Mrs. Terrence O. Kennedy in memory of her husband, Mr. Terrence O. Kennedy. 69.253

Dish with Design of Plover over Waves: Kyoto Ware. Glazed earthenware. Dish by Ogata Kenzan, 1663-1743, design by Ogata Korin, 1658-1716, Japanese, Edo period. W. 22. Purchase from the J. H. Wade Fund. 66.365

Highboy. Maple and walnut veneer. America, Massachusetts, ca. 1700-20. H. 158.5. Gift of Gordon D. and Jean F. Meals in memory of Moselle T. Meals. 86.207

Pier Glass with Frame (Trumeau). Carved and gilded wood. France, ca. 1715. H. 242.8. John L. Severance Fund. 53.153

Armchair. Carved wood and Savonnerie tapestry. France, ca. 1717. H. 122. John L. Severance Fund. 47.187

Study for "Le Conteur" (The Romancer). Red and black chalk, ca. 1716. Jean Watteau, French. H. 35. Dudley P. Allen Fund. 28.661

Pilgrim Bottle. Polished stoneware with silver-gilt mounts. Germany, Meissen, ca. 1715. H. 15.9. Purchase from the J. H. Wade Fund. 51.451

The Apotheosis of a Saint. Oil on canvas, ca. 1695. Sebastiano Ricci, Italian. H. 76.5. Mr. and Mrs. William H. Marlatt Fund. 80.39

Flounce (detail). Lace, *point de France;* linen. France, late 17th-early 18th c. Overall H. 63.5. Gift of Mrs. Edward S. Harkness in memory of Mrs. Stephen V. Harkness. 30.654

Minuet in a Pavillion. Oil on canvas, ca. 1730. Jean-Baptiste Pater, French. H. 55.3. Gift of Commodore Louis D. Beaumont. 38.392

Armoire. Tulipwood and kingwood, ca. 1720. Attr. to Charles Cressent, French. H. 247.6. John L. Severance Fund. 58.129

Spoon, Fork, and Knife. Gold. Germany, Augsburg, ca. 1725. Max. L. 22.2. John L. Severance Fund. 63.473-.475

The Risen Christ Appearing to the Virgin. Oil on canvas, ca. 1708. Francesco Solimena, Italian. H. 222.5. Mr. and Mrs. William H. Marlatt Fund. 71.63

Pan and Syrinx. Oil on canvas, 1720. Jean-François de Troy, French. W. 139. Mr. and Mrs. William H. Marlatt Fund. 73.212

David Victorious over Goliath. Terracotta, 1722. Giovanni Battista Foggini, Italian, Florence. H. 41.2. Gift of Harold T. Clark, in memory of Mrs. William B. Sanders. 66.126

Fish and Rocks. Handscroll, ink on paper. Zhu Da, Chinese, 1624-ca. 1705, Qing dynasty. W. 157.5. John L. Severance Fund. 53.247

Man Dhata in Yoga Posture. Color on paper. India, Pahari, Basohli school, ca. 1690-1700. H. 20. Edward L. Whittemore Fund. 66.27

Textile (detail). Lampas weave; silk. India, Jaipur school, 17th c. Overall W. 172.5. Gift of George P. Bickford. 53.474

Standing Figure of a Beauty: Kakiemon-type Ware. Porcelain with overglaze enamels. Japan, Edo period, late 17th c. H. 38. John L. Severance Fund. 64.366

Reminiscence of Qinhuai River. Eight-leaf album, ink and color on paper. Daoji (Shitao), Chinese, 1642-1707, Qing dynasty. H. 25.5. John L. Severance Fund. 66.31

Strolling Companions in the Autumn Mountains. Double album leaf mounted as a handscroll, ink and color on paper. Kuncan, Chinese, act. 2d half 17th c., Qing dynasty.

W. 64.4. Purchase from the J. H. Wade Fund. 66.367

The Heroine Who Is Faithfully Loved. From Bhanu Datta's *Rasamanjari.* Color on paper. India, Pahari, Nurpur school, ca. 1710. W. 28.3. Gift of Dr. and Mrs. Sherman E. Lee. 67.239

Woman as an Itinerant Monk: Onna Komuso. Hanging scroll, ink and color on paper. Japan, Edo period, late 17th-early 18th c. H. 60.7. Andrew R. and Martha Holden Jennings Fund. 83.9

Sugriva Challenges Bali. From the *Ramayana.* Color on paper. India, Pahari, Nurpur school, 1720. W. 30.9. Purchase from the J. H. Wade Fund. 73.103

Vase with Floral Petals. Porcelain with peach-bloom glaze. China, Qing dynasty, Kangxi mark and period, 1662-1722. H. 21.1. Bequest of John L. Severance. 42.669

Landscapes after Various Old Masters. After Ni Zan. Album, ink and color on paper, dated 1690. Mei Qing, Chinese, Qing dynasty. W. 44. John L. Severance Fund. 62.157

Figure of a Woman. Hanging scroll, ink and color on paper. Inscription by Hakuin Ekaku, 1685-1768. Japan, Edo period. H. 122.3. The Kelvin Smith Collection, given by Mrs. Kelvin Smith. 85.281

Monteith. Silver gilt, dated 1715-16. Benjamin Pyne, English. H. 27. Gift of Mr. and Mrs. Warren H. Corning. 65.467

Still Life with Herrings. Oil on canvas. Jean Siméon Chardin, French, 1699-1779. H. 41. Leonard C. Hanna, Jr., Fund. 74.1

Covered Vase. Porcelain. Germany, Meissen, ca. 1728-30. H. 37.4. Andrew R. and Martha Holden Jennings Fund. 86.10

A Young Woman Buying a Pink from a Young Man. Black chalk heightened with white, ca. 1720. Giovanni Battista Piazzetta, Italian. W. 54.9. Purchase from the J. H. Wade Fund. 38.387

Casket. For members of the Boncompagni-Ludovisi and Ottoboni families. Silver gilt, stone, and enamel. Italy, Rome, 1731. L. 22.8. John L. Severance Fund. 74.86

Celebrations of Krishna's Birth. From *Bhagavata Purana.* Color on paper. India, Pahari, Mankot school, ca. 1730. H. 22.9. John L. Severance Fund. 88.70

Kitchen Utensils with Leeks, Onion, and Eggs. Oil on canvas, 1734. Jean Siméon Chardin, French. W. 40.7. Leonard C. Hanna, Jr., Fund. 80.37

Gaming Table. Wood and ivory marquetry. Germany, Mainz, ca. 1735. H. 77.7. John L. Severance Fund. 53.284

Interior of a Synagogue. Oil on canvas, ca. 1735-40. Alessandro Magnasco, Italian, Genoa. W. 149. Purchase from the J. H. Wade Fund. 30.22

Tureen. Silver, 1735-38. Designed by Juste-Aurèle Meissonier, French. L. tureen 35, stand 45. Leonard C. Hanna, Jr., Fund. 77.182

The Supper at Emmaus. Oil on canvas, ca. 1735-40. Giovanni Battista Piazzetta, Italian, Venice. W. 141.2. Purchase from the J. H. Wade Fund. 31.245

Album of Landscapes, Flowers and Birds. Ten-leaf album, ink and color on silk. Fan Qi, Chinese, 1616-ca. 1695, Qing dynasty. W. 17.3. Purchase from the J. H. Wade Fund. 75.22

Dish with Bird on Peach Branch. Porcelain with *famille verte* decoration. China, Qing dynasty, Kangxi mark and period, 1662-1722. D. 20.7. Severance and Greta Millikin Collection. 64.213

Court Lady Holding a Sheng. Porcelain with *famille verte* decoration. China, Qing dynasty, Kangxi period, 1662-1722. H. 30.3. Severance and Greta Millikin Collection. 64.195

Lover's Visit. Hanging scroll, ink and color on silk. Tamura Suio, Japanese, act. ca. 1680-1730, Edo period. W. 82.3. The Kelvin Smith Collection, given by Mrs. Kelvin Smith. 85.275

Tall Bamboo and Distant Mountains. After Wang Meng. Hanging scroll, ink on paper, dated 1694. Wang Hui, Chinese, Qing dynasty. H. 79.4. John L. Severance Fund. 53.629

Cup Stand with Dragons in Waves. Porcelain with yellow glaze. China, Qing dynasty, Kangxi period, 1662-1722. L. 13.2. Severance and Greta Millikin Collection. 64.196

Vase with Birds and Beasts. Porcelain with *famille jeune* decoration. China, Qing dynasty, Kangxi period, 1662-1722. H. 43.2. Bequest of John L. Severance. 42.718

Irises. One of a pair of six-fold screens, ink and color on gold ground paper. Watanabe Shiko, Japanese, 1683-1755, Edo period. W. 334.3. Gift of the Norweb Foundation. 54.604

Portrait of An Qi. Hanging scroll, ink and color on paper, dated 1715. Wang Hui, Tu Luo, and Yang Jin, Chinese, Qing dynasty. H. 121.8. John L. Severance Fund. 71.17

Landscape. After Ni Zan. Hanging scroll, ink and color on paper, dated 1707. Wang Yuanqi, Chinese, Qing dynasty. H. 80.3. John L. Severance Fund. 54.583

Pilgrim Flask with Floral Scrolls. Porcelain with underglaze blue decoration. China, Qing dynasty, Yongzheng mark and period, 1723-35. H. 49.2. Severance and Greta Millikin Collection. 64.226

Dish with Two Cocks in Land-scape. Porcelain with *famille rose* overglaze enamel decoration. China, Qing dynasty, Yongzheng period, 1723-35. D. 15.2. Severance and Greta Millikin Collection. 64.200

Tsuta-no-Hosomichi: The Ivy Lane. Six-fold screen, ink and color on gold ground paper. Fukae Roshu, Japanese, 1699-1757, Edo period. W. 267.8. John L. Severance Fund. 54.127

United States **England** **Spain** **France**

Portrait of Mrs. Thomas Bulfinch. Oil on canvas, ca. 1733. John Smibert, American. H. 75.5. Hinman B. Hurlbut Collection. 3919.20

Mantel. Marble, ca. 1730. Design attr. to William Kent, English. H. 153.7. Elisabeth Severance Prentiss Fund. 44.472

Still Life with Fish, Bread and Kettle. Oil on canvas, ca. 1730-40. Luis Meléndez, Spanish. W. 48. Leonard C. Hanna, Jr., Fund. 83.97

Portrait of Cardinal Dubois. Oil on canvas, 1723. Hyacinthe Rigaud, French. H. 146.7. John L. Severance Fund. 67.17

Portrait of Anne Louis Goislard de Montsabert, Comte de Richebourg-le-Toureil. Oil on canvas, 1734. Nicolas de Largillierre, French. H. 80.6. Mr. and Mrs. William H. Marlatt Fund. 70.31

Portrait of Jean-Gabriel de La Porte du Theil. Oil on canvas, ca. 1738-40. Jacques-André-Joseph-Camelot Aved, French. H. 124.5. John L. Severance Fund. 64.89

Portrait of Charles Apthorp. Oil on canvas, 1748. Robert Feke, American. H. 127. Gift of The John Huntington Art and Polytechnic Trust. 19.1006

Tea Caddy. Silver gilt, 1741/2. Paul de Lamerie, English, London. H. 13.3. Thomas S. Grasselli Memorial Collection. 43.179

Cachepot. Soft paste porcelain. France, Paris, Villeroy Factory, ca. 1735-40. D. 19.4. John L. Severance Fund. 47.60

A View of the Waterfalls at Tivoli. Oil on canvas, 1737. Claude-Joseph Vernet, French. W. 172.6. Leonard C. Hanna, Jr., Fund. 84.175

Flight into Egypt: The Holy Family Embarking in a Small Boat. Pen and brown ink, brown wash, over black chalk, ca. 1730-35. Giovanni Battista Tiepolo, Italian. W. 44.6. Pur-

chase from the J. H. Wade Fund. 29.443

Sita in the Garden of Lanka with Ravana and His Demons. From the *Ramayana.* Gold and color on paper. India, Pahari, Guler school, ca. 1725. W. 84.5. Gift of George P. Bickford. 66.143

Conversation in Autumn. Hanging scroll, ink and color on paper, dated 1732. Hua Yan, Chinese, Qing dynasty. H. 115.3. John L. Severance Fund. 54.263

Martyrdom of St. Sebastian: Modello for an Altarpiece. Oil on canvas, ca. 1739. Giovanni Battista Tiepolo, Italian. H. 52.5. Delia E. Holden and L. E. Holden Funds. 46.277

The Fall of Simon Magus. Oil on canvas, ca. 1746. Pompeo Batoni, Italian. H. 183. John L. Severance Fund. 83.217

Inauguration Portraits of Emperor Qianlong, the Empress, and Eleven Imperial Consorts (detail). Handscroll, ink and color on silk, datable to 1736. Giuseppe Castiglione (Lang Shining), Italian, Chinese school, and others, Qing dynasty. Overall W. 688.3. John L. Severance Fund. 69.31

The Adoration of the Magi. Pen and brown ink, brown wash, over black chalk, ca. 1740-45. Giovanni Battista Tiepolo, Italian. H. 38.7. Dudley P. Allen Fund. 44.474

Radha and Krishna Seated on a Balcony. Color on paper. India, Pahari, Guler school, ca. 1760. H. 32.5. Gift of Clara Taplin Rankin. 86.61

The Fountain. Black, white, and red chalk, ca. 1736. François Boucher, French. H. 38.1. John L. Severance Fund. 52.529

Fountain of Venus. Oil on canvas, dated 1756. François Boucher, French. H. 232.5. The Thomas L. Fawick Memorial Collection. 79.55

Tall Clock (Regulateur). Boulle marquetry with gilt-bronze mounts, 1744. Jacques-Pierre Latz, French, Paris. H. 261.5. John L. Severance Fund. 49.200

The Presentation in the Temple. Pen and brown ink, brown wash, heightened with white, over black chalk, ca. 1770. François Boucher, French. H. 32.2. Gift of Leonard C. Hanna, Jr. 25.1005

Hare and a Leg of Lamb. Oil on canvas, dated 1742. Jean-Baptiste Oudry, French. H. 98.1. John L. Severance Fund. 69.53

Gilt Bronze Clock. France, ca. 1750. H. 93. John L. Severance Fund. 51.550

Wall Clock. Gilt bronze. France, ca. 1750-60. H. 116.8. John L. Severance Fund. 50.376

Covered Bowl. Soft paste porcelain. France, Vincennes, ca. 1745. H. 15.3. Purchase from the J. H. Wade Fund. 44.225

Laban Searching for His Household Gods. Oil on canvas, 1753. Gabriel Jacques de Saint-Aubin, French. W. 57.3. Gift of Ruth and Sherman E. Lee in memory of their parents, George B. and Inez W. Ward, and Emery and Adelia Lee. 65.548

Six Miniatures. Gouache on card, 1753. Louis Nicholas van Blarenberghe, French. *Box.* Gold, 1753-54. Jean Charles Ducrollay, French, Paris. H. 3.4. Gift of Mrs. Edward B. Greene. 57.412

Vase. Porcelain. Germany, Meissen, 1749. Gilt-bronze mounts. France, Paris, ca. 1750. H. 31.1. Purchase from the J. H. Wade Fund. 44.230

Interior of the Colonnade of St. Peter's at the Time of the Conclave. Oil on canvas, 1760s. Hubert Robert, French. H. 43. Mr. and Mrs. William H. Marlatt Fund. 76.97

Pair of Lappets, Joined (detail). Lace, *point d'Angleterre;* linen. Flanders, Brussels, 1730s-40s. Overall L. 119.4. Gift of Mrs. Edward S. Harkness, in memory of Mrs. Stephen V. Harkness. 45.84

Gilt-Bronze Dish. Germany(?), 2d quarter 18th c. H. 31.9. John L. Severance Fund. 55.69

View of the Piazza San Marco, Venice. Oil on canvas, ca. 1732. Canaletto, Italian, Venice. W. 232.5. Leonard C. Hanna, Jr., Fund. 62.169

Jar with Relief Design of Four Characters. Glazed porcelain with molded and carved decoration. Korea, Choson period, 18th c. H. 20. The Severance and Greta Millikin Purchase Fund. 81.3

The Thirty-Six Immortal Poets. Two-fold screen, ink and color on paper. Attr. to Tatebayashi Kagei, Japanese, act. ca. 1740-50, Edo period. W. 182.6. Mr. and Mrs. William H. Marlatt Fund. 60.183

House Altar. Carved and gilded wood, ca. 1735-40. Joseph Matthias Götz, German, Bavaria. H. 166.8. Leonard C. Hanna, Jr., Fund. 64.357

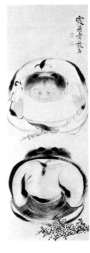

Interior of the Pantheon in Rome. Oil on canvas, 1747. Giovanni Paolo Panini, Italian. H. 127. Purchase from the J. H. Wade Fund. 74.39

Print Seller. Soft paste porcelain. Italy, Naples, Capo-di-Monte, ca. 1750. H. 20.3. Gift of Judge Irwin Untermyer. 50.570

The Large Boar Hunt. Pen and brown ink, gray wash heightened with white, 1747-48. Johann Wolfgang Baumgartner, German. W. 73.5. Dudley P. Allen Fund. 67.22

Kanzan and Jittoku. Hanging scroll, ink and color on paper. Ike Taiga, Japanese, 1723-76, Edo period. H. 121.5. Purchase from the J. H. Wade Fund. 79.49

Clock. Carved and gilded wood. Faience, ca. 1750. Works by Baumgartinger, Mergentheim, Germany. H. 97.8. John L. Severance Fund. 66.362

Imaginary View: A Palace on the Shore of the Lagoon. Pen and brown ink, gray wash, ca. 1755. Canaletto, Italian. W. 42.1. Purchase from the J. H. Wade Fund. 30.23

Hen and Chicks Tureen. Soft paste porcelain. England, Chelsea, ca. 1755. H. 24.8. Purchase from the J. H. Wade Fund. 84.58

Tureen with Platter. Faience. France, Strassbourg, ca. 1750. H. tureen 21.2. L. platter 38.6. Andrew R. and Martha Holden Jennings Fund. 76.52

Tureen. Soft paste porcelain. France, Vincennes, ca. 1752. H. 25.7. John L. Severance Fund. 52.3

Study for a Figure of Silence. Terracotta, early 1750s. Attr. to Jean-Baptiste Pigalle, French. H. 26.7. The Thomas L. Fawick Memorial Collection. 79.7

Commode. Oak, wood marquetry with gilt-bronze mounts, ca. 1750. Attr. to Jacques-Pierre Latz, French, Paris. H. 156.5. Gift of Flora Whitney Miller, Barbara Whitney Henry, and

Major Cornelius Vanderbilt Whitney, in memory of their mother, Mrs. Harry Payne Whitney. 42.497

Tureen. Soft paste porcelain. France, Vincennes-Sèvres, 1756. H. 24.2. John L. Severance Fund. 49.15

Tureen with Platter. Soft paste porcelain. France, Sèvres, 1757. H. tureen 24.2. L. platter 40.6. John L. Severance Fund. 53.25

Microscope. Gilt bronze. France, mid 18th c. H. 27.9. Purchase from the J. H. Wade Fund. 74.15

Table-Desk (Bureau Plat). Wood marquetry with gilt-bronze mounts, ca. 1750. Bernard van Risen Burgh II, French, Paris. H. 74.9. The Elisabeth Severance Prentiss Collection. 44.123

Monkey on a Dog. Soft paste porcelain. France, Mennecy, mid 18th c. H. 15.9. Gift of Rosenberg and Stiebel, Inc. 53.269

Tureen in the Form of a Pigeon. Faience. France, Sceaux, ca. 1760. H. 26.7. The Norweb Collection. 83.51

Tureen in the Form of a Basket of Game. Faience. France, Sceaux, ca. 1760. H. 20. The Norweb Collection. 83.52

Pair of Fire Dogs. Gilt bronze, 1752. Jacques Caffieri, French, Paris. H. 44.2. Bequest of John L. Severance. 42.799-.800

Portrait of François Tronchin. Pastel on parchment, 1757. Jean Etienne Liotard, Swiss. W. 46.3. John L. Severance Fund. 78.54

Presentation of Christ in the Temple. Oil on canvas, ca. 1750. Franz Anton Maulbertsch, Austrian. H. 69.5. Mr. and Mrs. William H. Marlatt Fund. 63.326

The Angels Appearing to Abraham (one of four). Oil on canvas. Giovanni Antonio Guardi, Italian, Venice, 1698-1760. W. 75.5. Mr. and Mrs. William H. Marlatt Fund. 52.237

Krishna Receives a Flower Garland. Color on paper. Sitaram, India, Rajasthan, Kishangarh school, ca. 1750-60. H. 42.3. John L. Severance Fund. 82.65

Vase with Dutchmen and Foreign Vessel: Arita Ware, Imari Type. Porcelain with overglaze enamel decoration. Japan, Edo period, 18th c. H. 55. Gift of Ralph King. 19.837

Christ at the Column. Gilt bronze, dated 1756. Johann Baptist Hagenauer, Austrian. H. 19.6. John L. Severance Fund. 53.286

Sake Bottle with Figure Designs: Arita Ware, Imari Type. Porcelain with overglaze enamel and gold decoration. Japan, Edo period, 18th c. H. 27.2. Severance and Greta Millikin Collection. 64.272

Dish with Reeds and Mist: Arita Ware, Nabeshima Type. Porcelain with underglaze blue and overglaze decoration. Japan, Edo period, ca. 18th c. D. 20.1. Severance and Greta Millikin Collection. 64.271

1698-1799

Portrait of Mrs. Anna Dummer Powell. Oil on canvas, 1764. John Singleton Copley, American. H. 126.6. Gift of Ellery Sedgwick, Jr., in memory of Mabel Cabot Sedgwick. 80.202

The Ladies Amabel and Mary Jemima Yorke. Oil on canvas, 1761. Sir Joshua Reynolds, English. H. 195.9. Bequest of John L. Severance. 42.645

Carpet. Knotted wool. France, Paris, Savonnerie Factory, ca. 1750. H. 620. John L. Severance Fund. 50.8

Candelabrum. Silver, 1758. François Thomas Germain, French, Paris. H. 38.1. Purchase from the J. H. Wade Fund. 40.14

La Marquise d'Aiguirandes. Oil on canvas, 1759. François Hubert Drouais. H. 101. Bequest of John L. Severance. 42.638

Portrait of Nathaniel Hurd. Oil on canvas, ca. 1765. John Singleton Copley, American. H. 76.2. Gift of The John Huntington Art and Polytechnic Trust. 15.534

The Elements: Air. Tapestry weave; silk, wool, and cotton. France, Paris, Gobelin Factory, 18th c. H. 353. Gift in memory of Mrs. Harry Payne Whitney. 42.495

Fête in a Park with Costumed Dancers. Pen and ink, gray wash and watercolor, over graphite, 1760-65. Gabriel Jacques de Saint-Aubin,

French. W. 31.3. Purchase from the J. H. Wade Fund. 66.124

Rectangular Box. Enamel on gold. France, Paris, 1768-69(?). H. 4.5. Gift of Mrs. Edward B. Greene. 57.410

George Pitt, First Lord Rivers. Oil on canvas, 1769. Thomas Gainsborough, English. H. 234.3. Gift of the John Huntington Art and Polytechnic Trust. 71.2

Portrait of Mrs. John Greene. Oil on canvas, 1769. John Singleton Copley, American. H. 125.5. Gift of The John Huntington Art and Polytechnic Trust. 15.527

Spring. Savonnerie panel. Ghiordes knot; silk and wool. France, Paris, Savonnerie Factory, 18th c. H. 138.9. John L. Severance Fund. 52.14

Candelabrum. Gilt bronze. Attr. to Jean Joseph de Saint-Germain, French, Paris, 1720-91. H. 72.4. John L. Severance Fund. 46.81

Bust of a Woman. Terracotta, 1770. Jean Baptiste Lemoyne II, French. H. 61.9. John L. Severance Fund. 52.566

Bust of Christoph Willibald Gluck. Terracotta, probably 1774. Jean-Antoine Houdon, French. H. 64. Leonard C. Hanna, Jr., Fund. 88.59

Fragment of a Carpet. Senna knot; wool and cotton. Northwestern Iran, 18th c. H.89. Purchase from the J. H. Wade Fund. 53.128

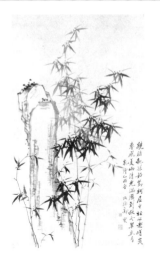

Young Woman Looking at a Pot of Pinks. Color woodblock print. Suzuki Harunobu, Japanese, 1724-70, Edo period. H. 27. The Kelvin Smith Collection, given by Mrs. Kelvin Smith. 85.304

Orpheus and Cerberus. Sandstone, ca. 1760-65. Ferdinand Tietz, German. H. 179.5. John L. Severance Fund. 71.65

Herm. Wood, late 1760s. Franz Ignaz Günther, German. H. 93.3. Purchase from the J. H. Wade Fund. 73.101

Bamboo and Rock. Hanging scroll, ink on paper, dated 1765. Zheng Xie, Chinese, Qing dynasty. H. 185.5. Mr. and Mrs. William H. Marlatt Fund. 82.54

Immaculate Conception. Polychromed and gilded wood, ca. 1765-70. Franz Ignaz Günther, German. H. 78.2. Leonard C. Hanna, Jr., Fund. 63.294

Kneeling Angel. Carved wood, ca. 1760s. Franz Ignaz Günther, German. H. 79.8. John L. Severance Fund. 66.18

Gathering at the Orchid Pavilion. Hanging scroll, ink on silk, dated 1777. Soga Shohaku, Japanese, Edo period. H. 122.5. Purchase from the J. H. Wade Fund. 79.53

Teapot. Silver. Nathaniel Hurd, American, Boston, 1729-77. H. 14.6. Gift of Hollis French. 40.228

Side Chair. Mahogany with needlework seat cover. America, New York, ca. 1760. H. 105.3. Leonard C. Hanna, Jr., Fund. 88.32

Scene with a Road Winding through a Wood. Pen and brown ink, and gray wash, 1770 or earlier. Thomas Gainsborough, British. W. 25.1. Dudley P. Allen Fund. 29.547

Punch Bowl. Soft paste porcelain. England, Worcester, ca. 1770. D. 27.6. Given in memory of John MacGregor, Jr., and Mary Folger MacGregor, by Mrs. John F. McGuire. 38.331

Sommeil, God of Sleep. Oil on canvas. French Master, 18th c. W. 130. Leonard C. Hanna, Jr., Fund. 63.502

Mrs. West and Her Son Raphael. Oil on canvas, ca. 1770. Benjamin West, American. W. 89.5. The Charles W. Harkness Gift. 27.393

George Washington at the Battle of Princeton. Oil on canvas, ca. 1780. Charles Willson Peale, American. H. 132. The Cleveland Museum of Art. 17.946

Woman Standing among the Friars (recto). Pencil, brush and black ink, and black and gray wash, 1770s. John Brown, British. W. 36.9. Dudley P. Allen Fund. 69.28

The Guilty and Repentant Daughter. Black chalk, gray wash and graphite, ca. 1770. Jean-Baptiste Greuze, French. W. 64.4. Leonard C. Hanna, Jr., Fund. 89.46

John, Lord Fitzgibbon. Oil on canvas, 1789. Gilbert Stuart, American. H. 245.1. General Income Fund. 19.910

Allegory. Pen and brown ink. John Mortimer, British, 1741-79. W. 36. Cornelia Blakemore Warner Fund and Delia E. Holden Fund. 78.20

View of Rome. Oil on paper mounted on pulp board. Pierre Henri de Valenciennes, French, 1750-1819. W. 38.9. Purchase from the J. H. Wade Fund. 70.55

A Basket of Plums. Oil on canvas, 1769. Anne Vallayer-Coster, French. W. 46.2. Mr. and Mrs. William H. Marlatt Fund. 71.47

Roman Ruins, Villa Pamfili. Pen and black ink, colored washes, heightened with white gouache, over black chalk, 1774. Hubert Robert, French. W. 44.5. Gift of Harry D. Kendrick. 51.485

Box. Gold and mother-of-pearl. Austria, Vienna(?), ca. 1765. H. 9.2. Gift of Mrs. A. Dean Perry. 67.157

Pluto. Porcelain, ca. 1760. Modeled by Franz Anton Bustelli, German, Munich, Nymphenburg Factory. H. 10.2. Gift of A. and R. Ball. 47.283

Miniature Mountain. Jade (nephrite). China, Qing dynasty, 18th c. H. 17.5. Anonymous Memorial Gift. 41.594

Oval Box. Gouache miniatures mounted in gold and enamel, dated 1779-80(?). Pierre Marie Gault de Saint-Germain, French, Paris. H. 3.4. Gift of Mrs. Edward B. Greene. 57.409

Work Table. Wood marquetry with gilt-bronze mounts. Sèvres porcelain top. Martin Carlin, French, Paris, act. 1766-85. H. 77.5. Bequest of John L. Severance. 42.594

Stool. Made for game room at Compiègne, but used at Fontainebleau. Carved wood, 1786-87. Jean-Baptiste-Claude Sené, French, Paris. H. 44.7. John L. Severance Fund. 54.385

Console Table. Made for Schloss Seehof, Franconia. Carved and gilded wood, ca. 1765. Attr. to Ferdinand Tietz, German. H. 85.7. John L. Severance Fund. 62.63

Paintings of Various Subjects: Su Wu Herding Sheep. Album, ink on paper, dated 1788. Min Zhen, Chinese, Qing dynasty. H. 29. John L. Severance Fund. 85.71

Portrait of a Boy (The Artist's Son?). Oil on panel, 1780s. Jean Honoré Fragonard, French. H. 21.2. Gift of Grace Rainey Rogers in memory of her father, William J. Rainey. 42.49

Invocation to Love. Brown wash, 1780-81. Jean Honoré Fragonard, French. W. 41.6. Grace Rainey Rogers Fund. 43.657

Count Tschernitscheff, Russian Ambassador at Vienna. Watercolor on ivory. Friedrich Heinrich Füger, German, 1751-1818. D. 10.1. Gift of Edward B. Greene. 42.1141

Brazier. Silver with wood handle and feet. John Potwine, American, Boston, 1698-1792. H. 8.2. Gift of Hollis French. 40.248

The Valley of Mawddach with Cader Idris. Oil on canvas, ca. 1775. Richard Wilson, British. W.105.5. Leonard C. Hanna, Jr., Fund. 89.52

Landscape with Figures. Pastel on prepared fabric, 1779. Jean Pillement, French. W. 61. Mr. and Mrs. William H. Marlatt Fund. 73.1

Candelabrum. Bronze and gray marble, ca. 1785. Claude Michel (called Clodion), French. H. 92.1. Gift of Grace Rainey Rogers in memory of her father, William J. Rainey. 42.59

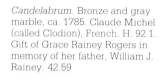

Side Chair. Mahogany. America, Philadelphia, Chippendale style, ca. 1770. H. 97. Leonard C. Hanna, Jr., Fund. 85.58

Rocky Wooded Landscape. Oil on canvas, ca. 1782-83. Thomas Gainsborough, English. W. 91. Mr. and Mrs. William H. Marlatt Fund. 84.59

Young Girl. Terracotta, ca. late 1770s. Claude Michel (called Clodion), French. H. 45. Gift of Grace Rainey Rogers in memory of her father, William J. Rainey. 42.50

Clock. Movement by Robert Robin. Case: Gilt bronze, ca. 1785. Robert Osmond, French. H. 62. John L. Severance Fund. 85.11

Boudoir from the Hotel d'Hocqueville. Carved and painted wood with plaster ceiling and ornamental reliefs, ca. 1785. France, Rouen. H. 409. John L. Severance Fund. 70.53

Mantel. Marble, ca. 1785. Probably designed by and executed in the studio of John Bacon, English. H. 152.4. Elisabeth Severance Prentiss Fund. 44.471

Armchair. Carved and gilded wood. Jacques-Jean-Baptiste Tilliard (called Jean Baptiste II Tilliard), French, Paris, act. 1752-97. H. 102.5. Purchase from the J. H. Wade Fund. 27.424

Hubert Robert. Terracotta, ca. 1780-90. Augustin Pajou, French. H. 71. Leonard C. Hanna, Jr., Fund. 87.8

Les plaisirs de la ferme. Copperplate printed cotton. France, Jouy-en-Josas, Oberkampf Manufactory, 1785-90. Designed by J. B. Huet. H. 196.9. Dudley P. Allen Fund. 28.5

Chest of Drawers. Ebony veneer, Japanese lacquer panels, gilt-bronze mounts. René Dubois, French, Paris, 1737-99. H. 86.9. The Elisabeth Severance Prentiss Collection. 44.113

Table. Mahogany, with gilt-bronze mounts and white marble top, ca. 1785. Adam Weisweiler, French, Paris. H. 91.5. Gift from an Anonymous Donor. 22.73

Desk. Mahogany, ca. 1790. David Roentgen, German. W. 174.7. Severance and Greta Millikin Collection. 64.297

God the Father. Polychromed wood, ca. 1775-85. Johann Peter Schwanthaler the Elder, Austrian. H. 142.2. Purchase from the J. H. Wade Fund. 61.30

St. Joachim. Polychromed and gilded wood. Follower of Joseph Anton Feuchtmayer, South German, 2d half 18th c. H. 129.4. Purchase from the J. H. Wade Fund. 62.246

Bitch with Her Litter. Color on paper. India, Rajasthan, Ajmer, probably Sawar, ca. 1780. W. 25.3. Gift of Mr. and Mrs. William E. Ward in memory of her father, Charles Svec. 69.77

Drunken Zhong Kui Supported by Ghosts. Hanging scroll, ink and color on paper. Luo Ping, Chinese, 1733-99, Qing dynasty. H. 96.8. Norman O. Stone and Ella A. Stone Memorial Fund. 59.185

1698-1799

Chair. Carved mahogany with
ebony feet, ca. 1800. Attr. to
Samuel McIntire, American,
Salem. H. 97.1. Purchase from
the J. H. Wade Fund. 62.125

*The Thought of Death Alone,
The Fear Destroys.* Graphite,
ca. 1795. William Blake, British.
W. 30.8. Gift of The Print Club of
Cleveland. 32.318

Armchair. Carved and partially
gilded boxwood. Nicholas-Denis
Delaisement, French, Paris, act.
1776-after 1792. H. 98.1. The
Elisabeth Severance Prentiss
Collection. 44.110

Straw Marquetry Desk. France,
3d quarter 18th c. H. 97.2. Gift
of Grace Rainey Rogers, in
memory of her father, William J.
Rainey. 42.40

Tambour Desk. Mahogany,
ca. 1800. John and Thomas
Seymour, American, Boston.
H. 104.4. Leonard C. Hanna, Jr.,
Fund. 87.11

*Mrs. Catharine Clemens and
Her Son, John Marcus Clemens.*
Watercolor on ivory. Richard
Cosway, English, 1742(?)-1821.
H. 8.3. Gift of Edward B.
Greene. 41.552

Infante Don Luis de Borbón. Oil
on canvas, 1783. Francisco
Goya y Lucientes (after Mengs).
H. 152.7. Leonard C. Hanna,
Jr., Fund. 66.14

Ecuelle. Porcelain, 1795. Enamel
decoration by Dodin, France,
Sèvres. Max. D 23.5. Sundry
Purchase Fund. 71.64

Lady Louisa Manners. Oil on
canvas, 1794. Thomas
Lawrence, English. H. 255.3.
Bequest of John D. Rockefeller,
Jr. 61.220

*The Daughters of Colonel
Thomas Carteret Hardy.* Oil on
canvas, ca. 1801. Thomas
Lawrence, English. H. 129.
Bequest of John L. Severance.
42.642

Tureen and Platter. Silver,
1798-1809. Henri Auguste,
French, Paris. H. tureen 26.2.
D. platter 49.2. Gift of James
Hazen Hyde. 52.592

Secretary. Mahogany with ormolu mounts, marble top, ca. 1800. Attr. to Bernard Molitor, French, Paris. H. 144.7. The Thomas L. Fawick Memorial Collection. 79.36

Visit of Pope Pius VI in Venice: Te Deum in the Church of SS. Giovanni e Paolo. Oil on canvas, 1782. Francesco Guardi, Italian, Venice. W. 69. Gift of the Hanna Fund. 49.188

Vase with Birds on Flowering Branch. Porcelain with overglaze enamel decoration. China, Qing dynasty, Qianlong mark and period, 1736-95. H. 19. John L. Severance Fund. 71.145

The Inconstant Type. From the series "Studies in Physiognomy," color woodblock print. Kitagawa Utamaro, Japanese, 1753-1806, Edo period. H. 36.2. Bequest of Edward L. Whittemore. 30.218

Gaudi Ragini. Color on paper. India, Rajasthan, Raghugarh school, ca. 1780-1800. H. 20.5. Edward L. Whittemore Fund. 75.40

Flower Stand. Wood and gilt bronze, ca. 1800. Mounts made by Pierre Philippe Thomire, French. H. 104.2. Gift of Carrie Moss Halle in memory of Salmon Portland Halle. 60.94

Hindola Raga. Color on paper. India, Pahari, Kangra school, ca. 1790-1800. H. 20.7. Edward L. Whittemore Fund. 75.9

Vase with Figures in Landscape. Porcelain with overglaze enamel decoration. China, Qing dynasty, Qianlong mark and period, 1736-95. H. 15.4. John L. Severance Fund. 63.514

Screen with European Travelers. Enamel on copper, with cast-iron stand. China, Qing dynasty, Qianlong period, 1736-95. H. 65.8. Severance and Greta Millikin Collection. 64.243

United States

Spain

France

Germany

A Hussar Officer on Horseback.
Black and white chalk,
ca. 1805-13. John Singleton
Copley, American. H. 27.5.
Norman O. Stone and Ella A.
Stone Memorial Fund. 50.216

St. Ambrose. Oil on canvas,
ca. 1797. Francisco Goya y
Lucientes, Spanish. H. 190.
Leonard C. Hanna, Jr., Fund.
69.23

La Citoyenne Crouzet. Oil on
canvas, ca. 1800. Circle of
Jacques Louis David, French.
H. 80. Grace Rainey Rogers
Fund. 43.659

*View from the Solfatara onto
the Gulf of Pozzuoli.* Oil on
canvas, 1803. Jacob Philipp
Hackert, German. W. 166.5.
Mr. and Mrs. William H. Marlatt
Fund. 83.14

Captain Jean T. David. Oil on
canvas, 1813. Thomas Sully,
American. H. 89.5. Gift of The
John Huntington Art and
Polytechnic Trust. 16.1979

*Landcape with Aqueduct and
Fortress.* Oil on canvas, 1807.
Jean Victor Bertin, French.
W. 40.8. Mr. and Mrs. William
H. Marlatt Fund. 85.35

Portrait of Samuel Williams. Oil
on canvas, ca. 1818. Washington Allston, American. H. 142.2.
Mr. and Mrs. William H. Marlatt
Fund. 65.474

*Portrait of Don Juan Antonio
Cuervo.* Oil on canvas, 1819.
Francisco Goya y Lucientes,
Spanish. H. 120. Mr. and Mrs.
William H. Marlatt Fund. 43.90

Cupid and Psyche. Oil on
canvas, 1817. Jacques Louis
David, French. W. 241.6.
Leonard C. Hanna, Jr., Fund.
62.37

Tiger Hunt. Color on paper.
India, Rajasthan, Kota school,
ca. 1800. L. 49.1. Gift of George
P. Bickford. 85.64

Diamond Mountains (detail).
Ten-panel screen, ink and color
on cloth. Korea, Choson period,
late 18th c. W. 438.2. Mr. and
Mrs. William H. Marlatt Fund.
89.6

Summer Night. One of a pair of
six-fold screens, ink, gold
and silver on paper. Maruyama
Okyo, Japanese, 1733-95,
Edo period. W. 362. Leonard C.
Hanna, Jr., Fund. 73.157

1733-1819

Ladies Hunting from a Pavilion.
Color and gold on paper. India,
Rajasthan, Kota school,
ca. 1810. H. 38.1. Purchase
from the J. H. Wade Fund. 55.48

*Scroll Box with Phoenix and
Dragon Design.* Lacquer on
wood with inlaid mother-of-
pearl and brass wire. Korea,
Choson period, late 18th c.

L. 87. The Severance and Greta
Millikin Purchase Fund. 90.15

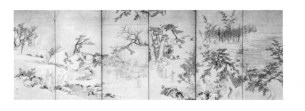

*Gathering at the Orchid
Pavilion.* Six-fold screen, ink and
slight color on paper. Maruyama
Okyo, Japanese, 1733-95, Edo
period. W. 191.8. John L.
Severance Fund. 77.1

*Jar with Bird and Flower
Design.* Porcelain with underglaze blue decoration. Korea,
Choson period, late 18th-early
19th c. H. 50.5. Gift of Yamanaka Shoji in memory of
Yamanaka Jiro. 89.117

Tiered Box with Stand. Wood
with colored lacquer and gold
and incised decoration. Japan,
Ryukyu Islands, late 18th c.
W. 68. Purchase from the J. H.
Wade Fund. 89.5

Poetic Gathering. Hanging
scroll, ink and color on paper.
Matsumura Goshun, Japanese,
1752-1811, Edo period. H. 106.4.
Andrew R. and Martha Holden
Jennings Fund. 83.188

Sir H. C. Englefield, Bart.
Marble, 1818. Sir Francis Legatt
Chantrey, English. H. 55.3.
Andrew R. and Martha Holden
Jennings Fund. 78.22

*The Disasters of War: And
There's No Help For It.* Etching,
drypoint, and engraving, 1810-
20, working proof. Francisco
Goya y Lucientes, Spanish.
W. 16.6. Leonard C. Hanna, Jr.,
Fund. 87.56

Les Révoltés du Caire. Oil on
paper pasted on canvas, 1810.
Anne-Louis Girodet de Roucy-
Trioson, French. W. 23.5. Gift of
Eugene Victor Thaw. 65.310

The Palace of the Doge, Venice.
Oil on mill board, 1826. Richard
Parkes Bonington, English.
W. 42.7. John L. Severance
Fund. 85.56

*The Bulls of Bordeaux: The
Famous American, Mariano
Ceballos.* Lithograph, 1825,
state II/II. Francisco Goya y
Lucientes, Spanish. W. 40.4.
Mr. and Mrs. Lewis B. Williams
Collection. 49.2

Panel. Lampas weave, bro-
caded, areas of embroidery; silk.
France, Lyon, Directoire period,
late 18th-early 19th c. H. 203.2.
Purchase from the J. H. Wade
Fund. 45.97

The Artist in His Room. Oil on
canvas, 1817. Léon Cogniet,
French. H. 44.2. Mr. and Mrs.
William H. Marlatt Fund. 78.51

*Portrait of Comte Jean-Antoine
Chaptal.* Oil on canvas, 1824.
Baron Antoine-Jean Gros,
French. H. 136.5. Leonard C.
Hanna, Jr., Fund. 64.54

Study of a Nude Woman, Seated Looking to the Right. Black and white chalk, ca. 1810. Pierre Paul Prud'hon, French. H. 61.9. Purchase from the J. H. Wade Fund. 61.318

Lateral panels for the "Bataille des Pyramides": *General Kléber* (left) and *Native Family* (right). Oil on canvas, 1810s. Baron Antoine-Jean Gros, French.

H. each 304.8. John L. Severance Fund. 72.17-.18

Duchess of Ragusa. Watercolor on vellum, 1818. Jean-Baptiste Isabey, French. W. 12.7. Gift of Edward B. Greene. 42.1146

Fighting Horses. Watercolor over graphite, ca. 1820. Théodore Géricault, French. W. 29.5. The Charles W. Harkness Endowment Fund. 29.13

Armored Figure on Horseback. Brown wash over graphite, 1828. Eugène Delacroix, French. W. 39.8. Dudley P. Allen Fund. 33.418

Napoleone Elisa Baciocchi. Marble, 1810-12. Lorenzo Bartolini, Italian. H. 113. The Thomas L. Fawick Memorial Collection. 79.37

Terpsichore. Marble, dated 1816. Antonio Canova, Italian. H. 177.5. Leonard C. Hanna, Jr., Fund. 68.212

Mountain Monkeys. Hanging scroll, ink and color on paper. Nagasawa Rosetsu, Japanese, 1754-99, Edo period. H. 164.4. Leonard C. Hanna, Jr., Fund. 85.192

Portrait of a Woman. Hanging scroll, ink and color on paper. Gion Seitoku, Japanese, 1781-1829, Edo period. H. 56.6. The Kelvin Smith Collection, given by Mrs. Kelvin Smith. 85.271

Tiger Family (detail). One of a pair of six-fold screens, ink and color on paper. Kishi Ganku, Japanese, 1749/56-1838, Edo period. Overall W. 362.5. Leonard C. Hanna, Jr., Fund. 83.4

Lintel. Wood. Polynesia, New Zealand, Maori, early to mid 19th c. H. 35. The Mary Spedding Milliken Memorial Collection, Gift of William Mathewson Milliken. 62.350

Breast Pendant. Wood. Polynesia, Rapa Nui (Easter Island), 19th c. L. 69.8. The Mary Spedding Milliken Memorial Collection, Gift of William Mathewson Milliken. 61.406

Gillett House Door. Painesville, Ohio. Wood, glass, and metal. Designed by Jonathon Goldsmith, American, 1783-1847. H. 292.5. Gift of Mrs. A. Dean Perry. 59.342

Console Table. Mahogany, ca. 1829-35. Joseph Meeks and Sons, American, New York. W. 105.5. Gift of Mrs. R. Livingston Ireland. 81.65

Branch Hill Pond, Hampstead Heath. Oil on canvas, 1828. John Constable, English. W. 78. Leonard C. Hanna, Jr., Fund. 72.48

The Roman Campagna. Oil on canvas, 1827. Jean-Baptiste-Camille Corot, French. W. 135.2. Leonard C. Hanna, Jr., Fund. 63.91

View of Florence from San Miniato. Oil on canvas, 1837. Thomas Cole, American. W. 160.3. Mr. and Mrs. William H. Marlatt Fund. 61.39

Burning of the Houses of Parliament, 1834. Oil on canvas, 1835. Joseph Mallord William Turner, English. W. 123.2. Bequest of John L. Severance. 42.647

Greek Pirates Attacking a Turkish Vessel. Oil on canvas, 1827. Eugène Isabey. W. 74.2. Gift of Mr. and Mrs. J. H. Wade. 16.1034

Schroon Mountain, Adirondacks. Oil on canvas, 1838. Thomas Cole, American. W. 160. Hinman B. Hurlbut Collection. 1335.17

Fluelen-Lake of Lucerne. Watercolor, 1840-45. Joseph Mallord William Turner, English. W. 47.9. Mr. and Mrs. William H. Marlatt Fund. 54.129

Antiochus and Stratonice. Oil on canvas, 1834. Jean Auguste Dominique Ingres, French. W. 63.5. Mr. and Mrs. William H. Marlatt Fund. 66.13

Portrait of Mme Raoul-Rochette. Graphite, 1830. Jean Auguste Dominique Ingres, French. H. 32.2. Purchase from the J. H. Wade Fund. 27.437

Portrait of Crescentia Countess Zichy (later Countess Szechenyi). Oil on canvas, 1828. Ferdinand Georg Waldmüller, Austrian. H. 97.8. John L. Severance Fund. 88.57

Two Mounted Huntsmen in a Landscape near Munich. Oil on panel, 1823. Wilhelm von Kobell, German. H. 25. Mr. and Mrs. William H. Marlatt Fund. 81.11

Club (U'u). Stained ironwood. Polynesia, Marquesas Islands, early 19th c. H. 148.3. James Albert and Mary Gardiner Ford Memorial Fund. 63.255

Portrait of Ozorabuzaemon. Hanging scroll, ink and color on paper, dated 1827. Watanabe Kazan, Japanese, Edo period. H. 221.3. Leonard C. Hanna, Jr., Fund. 80.177

Self-Portrait in His Studio. Oil on canvas, 1832. Emile-Jean Horace Vernet, French. H. 65. Mr. and Mrs. William H. Marlatt Fund. 77.171

Prater Landscape. Oil on panel, 1828. Ferdinand Georg Waldmüller, Austrian. W. 31. The Andrew R. and Martha Holden Jennings Fund. 83.155

Stilt Footrest. Wood. Polynesia, Marquesas Islands, early 19th c. H. 38.1. Gift of Mr. and Mrs. J. J. Klejman. 70.114

Mlle Julie de la Boutraye (later Comtesse Raymond du Tillet). Oil on canvas, 1834. Eugène Delacroix, French. H. 73. In Memory of Maud Stager Eells, gift from her daughter. 62.3

Landscape in the "Mi" Style. Hanging scroll, ink, color, and gold on paper. Tanomura Chikuden, Japanese, 1777-1840, Edo period. H. 175. The Kelvin Smith Collection, given by Mrs. Kelvin Smith. 85.250

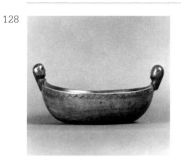

Bowl. Carved maple. Native American, Eastern Woodlands, Oneida, mid 19th c. W. 19.8. Purchase from the J. H. Wade Fund. 84.12

Lady Eastlake. Photograph, salt print from a calotype negative, ca. 1844-45. David Octavius Hill and Robert Adamson, British. H. 21.6. Andrew R. and Martha Holden Jennings Fund. 87.16

Study for Mehemet Ali Pasha. Watercolor and white gouache over black chalk, ca. 1844. John Frederick Lewis, British. H. 36.2. Mr. and Mrs. William H. Marlatt Fund. 86.78

Pasture Rose. Watercolor on vellum. Pierre Joseph Redouté, French, 1759-1840. H. 39.1. Gift in the name of Warren H. Corning from his wife and children. 59.15

Eskimo Girl. Oil on canvas. Léon Cogniet, French, 1794-1880. H. 42.5. Bequest of Noah L. Butkin. 80.249

Sideboard. Walnut. America, Philadelphia(?), ca. 1855, sculptural elements possibly executed by Joseph Alexis Bailly. H. 290.5. Purchase from the J. H. Wade Fund. 85.72

A Scene in York. Photograph, salt print from a calotype negative, 1845. William Henry Fox Talbot, British. W. 20.4. John L. Severance Fund. 84.163

Head of a Woman. Oil on canvas, 1844. Jean-Léon Gérôme, French. H. 44.5. Bequest of Noah L. Butkin. 80.264

Return from the Fields. Oil on canvas, ca. 1845-47. Jean-François Millet, French. H. 45.7. Mr. and Mrs. William H. Marlatt Fund. 72.19

The Eve of the Deluge. Oil on canvas, 1848. John Linnell, Sr., English. W. 223.5. Mr. and Mrs. William H. Marlatt Fund. 72.119

Fountain of Notre-Dame at St. Brieuc, Brittany. Photograph, salt print from a calotype negative, ca. 1850. Louis-Rémy Robert, French. H. 32.1. John L. Severance Fund. 84.17

Alexandre Dumas Père. Photograph, salt print, 1855. Nadar (Gaspard Félix Tournachon), French. H. 24.4. John L. Severance Fund. 83.198

Portrait of Dr. Johann Henning Kettil Hjardemaal. Oil on canvas, 1833. Christen Schjellerup Købke, Danish. H. 35.5. Mr. and Mrs. William H. Marlatt Fund. 87.51

Sophie Guillemette, Grand Duchess of Baden. Oil on canvas, 1830s. Franz Xavier Winterhalter, German. H. 39.5. The Thomas L. Fawick Memorial Collection. 79.43

Epidauros. Pen and black ink, watercolor, over graphite, 1843. Carl Rottmann, German. W. 43.9. John L. Severance Fund. 84.60

Worship of Sri Natha-ji. Temple hanging (*pechwai*), color on cloth. India, Rajasthan, Nathadwara school, 1825-50. H. 206. Purchase from the J. H. Wade Fund. 37.454

Fuji in Clear Weather. From the series "Thirty-Six Views of Mt. Fuji," color woodblock print. Katsushika Hokusai, Japanese, 1760-1849, Edo period. W. 37.5.

Bequest of Edward L. Whittemore. 30.189

Evening Rain on the Karasaki Pine. From the series "Eight Views of Omi Province," color woodblock print. Ando Hiroshige, 1797-1858, Edo period. W. 35.3. The Kelvin Smith Col-

lection, given by Mrs. Kelvin Smith. 85.312

Ichikawa Danjuro VII as Kan Shojo (Sugawara no Michizane, 845-903). From the series "Famous Kabuki Plays," color woodblock print with mica. Utagawa Kunisada, Japanese, 1786-1864, Edo period. H. 38. The Kelvin Smith Collection, given by Mrs. Kelvin Smith. 85.333

Forest Rocks. Oil on canvas, 1851. David Johnson, American. W. 53.3. Mr. and Mrs. William H. Marlatt Fund. 67.125

The Devil and Tom Walker. Oil on canvas, 1856. John Quidor, American. W. 87.3. Mr. and Mrs. William H. Marlatt Fund. 67.18

Center Table. Rosewood, marquetry, brass inlay, and gilding, ca. 1860. Attr. to the Gustave Herter Firm, American, New York. W. 143.2. Purchase from the J. H. Wade Fund. 84.39

Portrait of Geneo Scott. Oil on canvas, 1859. Eastman Johnson, American. W. 127. Mr. and Mrs. William H. Marlatt Fund. 65.475

View Near Newport. Oil on canvas, ca. 1860. John Frederick Kensett, American. W. 55.9. Mr. and Mrs. William H. Marlatt Fund. 46.255

Twilight in the Wilderness. Oil on canvas, 1860. Frederic Edwin Church, American. W. 162.6. Mr. and Mrs. William H. Marlatt Fund. 65.233

Landscape with Hay Wain. Oil on canvas, 1861. Worthington Whittredge, American. W. 78.5. Mr. and Mrs. William H. Marlatt Fund. 75.20

The Briarwood Pipe. Oil on canvas, 1864. Winslow Homer, American. H. 42.9. Mr. and Mrs. William H. Marlatt Fund. 44.524

Odalisque. Oil on canvas. France, mid-19th c. W. 92. Gift of Leonard C. Hanna, Jr. 39.63

Coast near Villerville. Oil on canvas, 1855. Charles François Daubigny, French. W. 116. Bequest of William G. Mather. 51.323

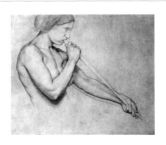

Study for an Angel Blowing a Trumpet. Black chalk, ca. 1855-57. Hilaire-Germain Edgar Degas, French. W. 54.2. Gift of The Print Club of Cleveland. 76.130

Un Effet de Soleil. Photograph, albumen print from a waxed paper negative, ca. 1856. Gustave LeGray, French. W. 41.8. Leonard C. Hanna, Jr., Fund. 87.54

Halt of the Greek Cavaliers. Oil on canvas, 1858. Eugène Delacroix, French. W. 61.5. Gift of Mr. and Mrs. J. H. Wade. 16.1032

Untitled (Waterfall in the Bois de Boulogne). Photograph, albumen print from a wet collodion negative, 1859. Charles Marville, French. W. 35.9. James E. Parmelee Fund. 89.27

Pierrot en correctionelle. Oil on panel. Thomas Couture, French, 1815-79. W. 38.1. Bequest of Noah L. Butkin. 80.250

Mme Laure Borreau (La Dame au Chapeau noir). Oil on canvas, dated 1863. Gustave Courbet, French. H. 81. Leonard C. Hanna, Jr., Fund. 62.2

Mlle Romaine Lacaux. Oil on canvas, 1864. Pierre Auguste Renoir, French. H. 81. Gift of the Hanna Fund. 42.1065

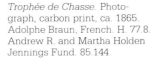

Setting Sun (Soleil couchant). Oil on canvas. Pierre-Etienne-Theodore Rousseau, French, 1812-67. W. 130.2. John L. Severance Fund. 83.70

Trophée de Chasse. Photograph, carbon print, ca. 1865. Adolphe Braun, French. H. 77.8. Andrew R. and Martha Holden Jennings Fund. 85.144

A Home in the Wilderness. Oil on canvas, 1866. Sanford Robinson Gifford, American. W. 77.5. Mr. and Mrs. William H. Marlatt Fund; The Butkin Foundation;

Dorothy Burnham Everett Memorial Collection, and various donors by exchange. 70.162

Half Dome, Yosemite Valley. Oil on canvas, 1866. Albert Bierstadt, American. W. 142.2. Hinman B. Hurlbut Collection. 221.22

Portrait of Mrs. Susanna Rose. Oil on panel, dated 1862. Frederick Sandys, English. H. 34.9. Mr. and Mrs. William H. Marlatt Fund. 79.81

David: "Oh, that I had the Wings of a Dove!" Oil on canvas, ca. 1865. Frederic, Lord Leighton of Stretton, English. W. 122.5. Leonard C. Hanna, Jr., Fund. 86.74

Point Judith, Rhode Island. Oil on canvas, ca. 1867. Martin Johnson Heade, American. W. 128. Mr. and Mrs. William H. Marlatt Fund. 70.161

Capri. Oil on canvas, 1869. William Stanley Haseltine, American. W. 80.2. Mr. and Mrs. William H. Marlatt Fund. 75.4

Glaucus and Nydia. Oil on wood panel, dated 1867. Sir Lawrence Alma-Tadema, English. W. 64.2. Gift of Mr. and Mrs. Noah L. Butkin. 77.128

Biglin Brothers Turning the Stake. Oil on canvas, 1873. Thomas Eakins, American. W. 153. Hinman B. Hurlbut Collection. 1984.27

Portrait of Mrs. George Waugh. Oil on canvas. William Holman Hunt, English, 1827-1910. H. 86.2. Mr. and Mrs. William H. Marlatt Fund. 84.41

Julia Jackson Duckworth. Photograph, albumen print from a wet collodion negative, 1874. Julia Margaret Cameron, British. H. 36.5. John L. Severance Fund. 84.165

The Guitarist. Etching on brown paper, 1861, state I/V. Edouard Manet, French. H. 30.9. The Fanny Tewksbury King Collection. 56.747

Connoisseurs. Watercolor, charcoal, and graphite, ca. 1862-64. Honoré Daumier, French. H. 26.2. Dudley P. Allen Fund. 27.208

The Troubador. Oil on canvas. Honoré Daumier, French, 1808-79. H. 83.2. Bequest of Leonard C. Hanna, Jr. 58.23

The Little Milkmaid. Oil on canvas. Théodule Augustin Ribot, French, 1823-91. H. 46. Mr. and Mrs. William H. Marlatt Fund. 73.31

Spring Flowers. Oil on canvas, 1864. Claude Oscar Monet, French. H. 116.9. Gift of the Hanna Fund. 53.155

Head of a Woman. Graphite, 1866. Adolph Menzel, German. H. 19.8. Andrew R. and Martha Holden Jennings Fund. 76.21

Portrait of Berthe Morisot. Oil on canvas, ca. 1869. Edouard Manet, French. H. 73.6. Bequest of Leonard C. Hanna, Jr. 58.34

On the Lookout (Sur un Belvedere). Oil on panel, dated 1867. Jean-Louis-Ernest Meissonier, French. H. 30.2. Bequest of Clara Louise Gehring Bickford. 86.68

Ville-d'Avray. A Peasant Cutting Reeds in a Swamp. Oil on canvas. Jean Baptiste Camille Corot, French, 1796-1875. W. 99. The Elisabeth Severance Prentiss Collection. 44.80

La Capeline Rouge—Mme Monet. Oil on canvas, ca. 1870. Claude Oscar Monet, French. H. 100.3. Bequest of Leonard C. Hanna, Jr. 58.39

The Artist's Sister, Mme Pontillon, Seated on the Grass. Oil on canvas, 1873. Berthe Morisot, French. W. 72.4. Gift of the Hanna Fund. 50.89

Bordeaux: Boats in the Port. Oil on canvas, 1874. Eugène Boudin, French. W. 89.5. John L. Severance Fund and Gift of Mrs. Dudley S. Blossom, Jr. 86.73

Vase with Portrait of President MacMahon. Porcelain with gilt-bronze mounts, 1872-74. Alfred-Thompson Gobert and Jules Archelais (decorators), Emile-Bernard Rejoux (gilder), Jean-

Denis Larue (sculptor), Constantin Renard (thrower), French, Sèvres. H. 89.2. The Thomas L. Fawick Memorial Collection. 79.40

The Clambake. Watercolor, 1873. Winslow Homer, American. W. 35.2. Gift of Mrs. Homer H. Johnson. 45.229

Center Table. Rosewood inlaid with other woods and bone, ca. 1875. Herter Brothers, American, New York. W. 122. John L. Severance Fund. 87.53

The Venetian Girl. Oil on canvas, ca. 1878. Frank Duveneck, American. H. 86.4. Gift of Mrs. Henry A. Everett for the Dorothy Burnham Everett Memorial Collection. 22.173

Budding Sycamore. Wash and gouache over graphite, 1875. John Ruskin, British. W. 44.8. Andrew R. and Martha Holden Jennings Fund. 89.14

Portrait of the Duchess of Montejasi-Cicerale. Oil on canvas, 1868. Hilaire-Germain Edgar Degas, French. H. 48.9. Bequest of Leonard C. Hanna, Jr. 58.28

Pointe de Cabellou, Coast of Brittany. Oil on canvas, 1881. William Picknell, American. W. 92.2. Purchase from the J. H. Wade Fund. 84.13

Ladle. Horn, bone, copper, abalone shell inlay. Native American, Northwest Coast, Tlingit, late 19th c. L. 30.5. The Harold T. Clark Educational Extension Fund. 53.386

Bowl Basket. Native American, California, Panamint, late 19th c. D. 43.2. Presented by William Albert Price in memory of his wife, Mrs. William Albert Price. 17.499

Tulips. Tabby ground, roller printed; cotton. England, 1875. Designed by William Morris. H. 76.1. Gift of Mrs. Philip T. White. 37.579

Race Horses. Pastel on cardboard, ca. 1873-75. Hilaire-Germain Edgar Degas, French. W. 65.4. Bequest of Leonard C. Hanna, Jr. 58.27

Leaping Trout. Watercolor, 1889. Winslow Homer, American. W. 50.2. Anonymous Gift. 73.142

Currecanti Needle, Black Canon of the Gunnison. Photograph, albumen print from a wet collodion negative, ca. 1883. William Henry Jackson, American. H. 53.5. Leonard C. Hanna, Jr., Fund. 85.45

Ceremonial Blanket. Mountain-goat wool, cedar bark. Native American, Northwest Coast, Tlingit, late 19th c. W. 162.5. Gift of Mr. and Mrs. Robert H. McGrath. 55.614

Portrait of Diego Martelli. Charcoal and white chalk, ca. 1879. Hilaire-Germain Edgar Degas, French. H. 44. John L. Severance Fund. 53.268

Bust of a Lady. Marble, dated 1872. Jean-Baptiste Carpeaux, French. H. 83.2. John L. Severance Fund. 75.5

Bust of a Lady. Terracotta, dated 1875. Jules Dalou, French. H. 64.1. Norman O. Stone and Ella A. Stone Memorial Fund. 67.31

The Lock at Pontoise (L'ecluse à Pontoise). Oil on canvas, dated 1872. Camille Pissarro, French. W. 83. Leonard C. Hanna, Jr., Fund. 90.7

Hannya Retrieving Her Arm. Hanging scroll, ink on paper. Shibata Zeshin, Japanese, 1807-91, Edo period. W. 172.2. Mr. and Mrs. William H. Marlatt Fund. 90.6

Otsu-e Subjects. Eight-fold screen, ink and color on cotton fabric. Shibata Zeshin, Japanese, 1807-91, Edo period. W. 395. John L. Severance Fund. 82.9

Grand Panorama of the Alps with the Dents du Midi. Oil on canvas, ca. 1875. Gustave Courbet, French. W. 209. John L. Severance Fund and various Donors by Exchange. 64.420

Le Fond de L'Hermitage. Oil on canvas, dated 1879. Camille Pissarro, French. W. 163.2. Gift of the Hanna Fund. 51.356

Mary Cassatt at the Louvre: The Paintings Gallery. Etching, softground etching, aquatint, and drypoint, 1879-80, state XV/XX, unique. Hilaire-Germain Edgar Degas, French. H. 30.2. The Charles W. Harkness Endowment Fund. 29.876

Frieze of Dancers. Oil on canvas, ca. 1883. Hilaire-Germain Edgar Degas, French. W. 200.6. Gift of the Hanna Fund. 46.83

Window. Leaded glass, ca. 1900-01. Louis Comfort Tiffany, American. H. 227.2. Gift of Mrs. Robert M. Fallon. 66.432

Portrait of Miss Dora Wheeler. Oil on canvas, 1883. William Merritt Chase, American. W. 165.8. Gift of Mrs. Boudinot Keith in memory of Mr. and Mrs. J. H. Wade. 21.1239

Jar. Earthenware. Native American, New Mexico, Zuñi Pueblo, late 19th c. H. 26. Gift of The Smithsonian Institution. 23.1082

Tray Basket. Native American, Arizona, Pima, late 19th c. W. 69.6. Bequest of Mrs. Horace Kelley. 29.274

Shinnecock Hills. Oil on canvas, ca. 1895. William Merritt Chase, American. W. 127. Gift of Mrs. Henry White Cannon. 38.333

Poplars on a Hill. Oil on canvas, 1889. Vincent van Gogh, Dutch, French school. H. 61. Bequest of Leonard C. Hanna, Jr. 58.32

The Road Menders at St. Remy. Oil on canvas, 1889. Vincent van Gogh, Dutch, French school. W. 92.1. Gift of the Hanna Fund. 47.209

Mlle Ravoux. Oil on canvas, 1890. Vincent van Gogh, Dutch, French school. H. 50.2. Bequest of Leonard C. Hanna, Jr. 58.31

The Age of Bronze. Bronze, 1876. Auguste Rodin, French. H. 180.8. Gift of Mr. and Mrs. Ralph King. 18.328

The Laundress. Brush and black ink, opaque white, ca. 1888. Henri de Toulouse-Lautrec, French. H. 76.2. Gift of the Hanna Fund. 52.113

The Thinker. Bronze. Auguste Rodin, French. H. 72.3. Gift of Alexandre P. Rosenberg. 79.138

Café Concert. Conté crayon with touches of white gouache, ca. 1887. Georges Seurat, French. H. 31.4. Leonard C. Hanna, Jr., Fund. 58.344

Monsieur Boileau at the Café. Gouache, 1893. Henri de Toulouse-Lautrec, French. H. 80. Hinman B. Hurlbut Collection. 394.25

Mother and Children. Oil on canvas. William Adolphe Bouguereau, French, 1825-1905. H. 164.5. Hinman B. Hurlbut Collection. 432.15

Mme Henry Lerolle and Daughter Yvonne. Oil on canvas, 1879-80. Albert Besnard, French. H. 165. Gift of Mr. and Mrs. Noah L. Butkin. 77.120

Portrait of Mme Henry Lerolle. Oil on canvas, 1882. Henri Fantin-Latour, French. H. 108.6. Purchase from the J. H. Wade Fund and the Fanny Tewksbury King Collection. 69.54

Covered Jar. Earthenware, dated 1885. Designed by Theodorus A. C. Colenbrander, Dutch, made by the Rozenburg Factory, The Hague. H. 39. Andrew R. and Martha Holden Jennings Fund. 86.60

Canoe Splashboard. Wood. Melanesia, New Guinea, Massim Area, Trobriand Islands, 19th c. H. 58.7. Gift of Mr. and Mrs. J. J. Klejman. 66.130

Beauty before a Screen. Hanging scroll, ink and color on silk. Kawanabe Kyosai, Japanese, 1831-89, Edo period. H. 144.2. The Kelvin Smith Collection, given by Mrs. Kelvin Smith. 85.268

Antibes. Oil on canvas, 1888. Claude Oscar Monet, French. W. 118.1. Gift of Mr. and Mrs. J. H. Wade. 16.1044

The Apple Seller. Oil on canvas, ca. 1890. Pierre Auguste Renoir, French. H. 65.7. Bequest of Leonard C. Hanna, Jr. 58.47

Ancestral Figure. Painted wood with fiber and tapa cloth. Melanesia, Papua New Guinea, Middle Sepik River, 19th c. H. 105.4. Gift of Dr. and Mrs. Thomas Munro. 71.150

Miss Loie Fuller. Lithograph, 1893. Henri de Toulouse-Lautrec, French. H. 37.9. Gift of Ralph King. 25.1202

May Belfort. Oil on cardboard, 1895. Henri de Toulouse-Lautrec, French. H. 62.9. Bequest of Leonard C. Hanna, Jr. 58.54

Three Bathers. Oil on canvas, 1897. Pierre Auguste Renoir, French. Purchase from the J. H. Wade Fund. 39.269

Sunny Autumn Day. Oil on canvas, 1892. George Inness, American. W. 106. Anonymous Gift. 56.578

Card Rack with Jack of Hearts. Oil on canvas, after 1894. John Frederick Peto, American. H. 76.2. Purchase from the J. H. Wade Fund. 73.30

Fifth Avenue Nocturne. Oil on canvas, ca. 1895. Childe Hassam, American. H. 61.2. Anonymous Gift. 52.538

Alarmus and Excursions. Pen and India ink, India wash with Chinese white, over pencil, 1899. Maxfield Parrish, American. H. 27.9. Bequest of James Parmelee. 40.723

Breastplate. Rawhide, quills, feathers, and metal cones. Native American, Lakota Sioux, ca. 1900. H. 44.5. Gift of Amelia Elizabeth White. 37.859

The Fitting. Drypoint and aquatint, 1890-91, state VI/VII. Mary Cassatt, American, French school. H. 37.6. Bequest of Charles T. Brooks. 41.72

After the Bath. Pastel, ca. 1901. Mary Cassatt, American, French school. W. 99.7. Gift of J. H. Wade. 20.379

Summer. Oil on canvas, dated 1891. Pierre Puvis de Chavannes, French. W. 232.5. Gift of Mr. and Mrs. J. H. Wade. 16.1056

Dancer Looking at Sole of Her Right Foot. Bronze, 1896-97. Hilaire-Germain Edgar Degas, French. H. 45.7. Hinman B. Hurlbut Collection. 2028.47

Ballet Girls. Pastel on paper, pasted on cardboard, 1897. Hilaire-Germain Edgar Degas, French. H. 55.3. Gift of Mr. and Mrs. J. H. Wade. 16.1043

The Pigeon Tower at Belle-vue. Oil on canvas, 1894-96. Paul Cézanne, French. W. 80. The James W. Corrigan Memorial. 36.19

Breaking Up City Hall Street (Doorbraak Raadhuisstraat, Amsterdam). Oil on canvas, 1895-96. George Hendrik Breitner, Dutch. W. 80.7. Mr. and Mrs. William H. Marlatt Fund. 85.145

The Jewish Boy. Wax, 1892-93. Medardo Rosso, Italian. H 22.2. Andrew R. and Martha Holden Jennings Fund. 70.33

Mask. Painted wood. Africa, Zaire, Kuba, ca. late 19th c. H. 43.2. James Albert and Mary Gardiner Ford Memorial Fund. 35.304

La Montagne Sainte-Victoire. Oil on canvas, 1894-1900. Paul Cézanne, French. W. 92.1. Bequest of Leonard C. Hanna, Jr. 58.21

The Brook. Oil on canvas, 1898-1900. Paul Cézanne, French. W. 80.7. Bequest of Leonard C. Hanna, Jr. 58.20

Bareback Rider. Monotype, ca. 1895. Maurice Prendergast, American. H. 25.4. Dudley P. Allen Fund. 54.362

Woman in the Waves (Ondine). Oil on canvas, dated 1889. Paul Gauguin, French. H. 92. Gift of Mr. and Mrs. William Powell Jones. 78.63

La Terrasse de Café. Oil on cardboard, 1898. Pierre Bonnard, French. W. 48. Anonymous Gift. 76.148

Under the Trees. Tempera on canvas, dated 1894. Edouard Vuillard, French. H. 214.6. Gift of the Hanna Fund. 53.212

May Day, Central Park. Watercolor, 1901. Maurice Prendergast, American. W. 50.6. Gift from J. H. Wade. 26.17

Head of a Tahitian Woman. Graphite, ca. 1891. Paul Gauguin, French. H. 30.6. Mr. and Mrs. Lewis B. Williams Collection. 49.439

Nursemaid's Promenade with Frieze of Carriages. Four lithographs, 1899. Pierre Bonnard, French. H. each sheet ca. 136.2. Leonard C. Hanna, Jr., Fund. 85.23-.26

L'Appel (The Call). Oil on canvas, dated 1902. Paul Gauguin, French. H. 130.2. Gift of the Hanna Fund. 43.392

The Café Wepler. Oil on canvas, ca. 1905. Edouard Vuillard, French. W. 103.2. Gift of the Hanna Fund. 50.90

Side Chair. Pearwood with tooled leather back and seat, ca. 1900. Designed by Hector Guimard, French. H. 108. Leonard C. Hanna, Jr., Fund. 85.96

Evening (Melancholia: On the Beach). Woodcut colored by hand, 1896, unique. Edvard Munch. W. 45. Gift of Mrs. Clive Runnells in memory of Leonard C. Hanna, Jr. 59.82

Figure. Wood, lizard skin, tooth, shell, and cloth. Africa, Zaire, Yaka, ca. 1900. Gift of Katherine C. White. 74.201

Ceremonial Adze. Wood, stone, and fiber. Polynesia, Mangaia, Cook Islands, 19th c. H. 124.5. Gift of Richard Inglis. 40.1078

Hand Mirror. Gold, enamel, and ivory, 1900. Designed by Felix Bracquemond, relief by Auguste Rodin, goldsmith: Falize Firm, French. H. 32.2. Gift of Ralph King, by Exchange. 78.43

The Vengeance of Hop-Frog. Etching, 1898, state II/II. James Ensor, Belgian. H. 35.9. Delia E. Holden Fund and L. E. Holden Fund. 70.38

Stone Pine and Alpine Roses. Oil on canvas, ca. 1897. Giovanni Segantini, Swiss. H. 136. Mr. and Mrs. William H. Marlatt Fund. 82.124

The Sin. Lithograph, 1901, state II/IV, proof. Edvard Munch, Norwegian. H. 69.8. Andrew R. and Martha Holden Jennings Fund. 83.185

Male Figure. Wood. Africa, Zaire, Yaka, ca. 1900. H. 61. James Albert and Mary Gardiner Ford Memorial Fund. 70.34

Hair Ornament. Horn, enamel, and gold, ca. 1900. René Lalique, French, Paris. H. 15.4. Gift of Mrs. A. Dean Perry. 81.49

1889-1905

Early Morning after a Storm at Sea. Oil on canvas, 1902. Winslow Homer, American. W. 127. Gift from J. H. Wade. 24.195

The Boat Builder. Oil on canvas, ca. 1904. John George Brown, American. W. 101.6. Hinman B. Hurlbut Collection. 905.72

La Vie. Oil on canvas, 1903. Pablo Picasso, Spanish, French school. H. 196.5. Gift of the Hanna Fund. 45.24

The Drive, Central Park. Oil on canvas, ca. 1905. William J. Glackens, American. W. 81.3. Purchase from the J. H. Wade Fund. 39.524

Maine Coast. Oil on canvas, 1907. Rockwell Kent, American. W. 112.4. Hinman B. Hurlbut Collection. 1132.22

Head of a Boy. Gouache, 1905. Pablo Picasso, Spanish, French school. H. 31. Bequest of Leonard C. Hanna, Jr. 58.43

Building a Dam, Shetucket. Oil on canvas, 1908. J. Alden Weir, American. W. 101.6. Purchase from the J. H. Wade Fund. 27.171

Stag at Sharkey's. Oil on canvas, 1909. George Bellows, American. W. 122.5. Hinman B. Hurlbut Collection. 1133.22

Figures in Pink. Oil on canvas, 1906. Pablo Picasso, Spanish, French school. H. 154.3. Bequest of Leonard C. Hanna, Jr. 58.45

Easter Egg. Lapis lazuli, gold, pearls, rubies, diamonds, enamel, ca. 1900. Firm of Carl Fabergé, Russian, St. Petersberg. H. 5.9. The India Early Minshall Collection. 66.436

Miniature Bidet. Gold, jade, enamel, and pearls, after 1903. Firm of Carl Fabergé; Henrik Wigström, workmaster. H. 8.3. The India Early Minshall Collection. 66.455

Mask. Wood and pigment. Africa, Cameroon, Kom, ca. 1900. L. 63.5. Gift of Mr. and Mrs. William D. Wixom in memory of Mr. and Mrs. Ralph M. Coe. 71.66

Tapis (sarong) (detail). Ikat and embroidery; cotton and silk. Indonesia, Southern Sumatra, Lampong, 19th c. Overall H. 130. Dudley P. Allen Fund. 83.215

The Houses of Parliament and Westminster Bridge. Oil on canvas, 1906. André Derain, French. W. 92.1. Leonard C. Hanna, Jr., Fund. 83.67

Mask. Wood, brass, and pigment, ca. 1900. Sabarikwo of Quazumon, African, Senufo, Ivory Coast. H. 31.1. John L. Severance Fund. 89.48

Cabinet. Wood marquetry with metal mounts, ca. 1910. Louis Majorelle, French. W. 162.6. John L. Severance Fund. 76.53

Tea Set. Silver and ivory, ca. 1910. Carlo Bugatti, Italian. W. 77.3. The Thomas L. Fawick Memorial Collection. 80.74-.78

Male Figure. Wood. Africa, Cameroon, Bangwa, ca. 1900. H. 92.1. Purchase from the J. H. Wade Fund. 87.62

The Race Track or *Death on a Pale Horse*. Oil on canvas, ca. 1910. Albert Pinkham Ryder, American. W. 89.5. Purchase from the J. H. Wade Fund. 28.8

Woman's Work. Oil on canvas, ca. 1911. John Sloan, American. H. 80.3. Gift of Amelia Elizabeth White. 64.160

Easter Monday—Hélène Daurment. Oil on canvas, 1906. Walter Sickert, British. H. 50.8. Mr. and Mrs. William H. Marlatt Fund. 82.145

Fan, Salt Box, Melon. Oil on canvas, 1909. Pablo Picasso, Spanish, French school. H. 81.3. Leonard C. Hanna, Jr., Fund. 69.22

Amorpha, Fugue in Two Colors II. Oil on canvas, 1910-11. Frantisek (Frank) Kupka, Czechoslovakian, French school. H. 111.7. Contemporary Collection of The Cleveland Museum of Art. 69.51

Holiday on the Hudson. Oil on canvas, ca. 1912. George Benjamin Luks, American. W. 91.7. Hinman B. Hurlbut Collection. 2291.33

Military. Oil on canvas, 1915. Marsden Hartley, American. H. 60.6. Jointly owned by The Cleveland Museum of Art and a private collector. 81.83

Self-Portrait. Oil and collage on panel, 1912. Sir William Orpen, British. H. 61. Mr. and Mrs. William H. Marlatt Fund. 88.11

Bottle, Glass, and Fork. Oil on canvas, 1912. Pablo Picasso, Spanish, French school. H. 74.5. Leonard C. Hanna, Jr., Fund. 72.8

Detachable Figure (Dancer). Ebony and oak, 1915. Jacques Lipchitz, American (b. Lithuania). H. 98.1. Gift of Mrs. Aye Simon. 72.367

Vase. Glass, 1915. Louis Comfort Tiffany, American. H. 19.9. Norman O. Stone and Ella A. Stone Memorial Fund. 70.126

Rodin Working on the Gates of Hell. Bronze, 1910. Emile Antoine Bourdelle, French. H. 68.3. Gift of A. M. Luntz. 43.291

Portrait of Mlle Violette Heymann. Pastel, dated 1910. Odilon Redon, French. W. 92.5. Hinman B. Hurlbut Collection. 1976.26

Wrestlers in a Circus. Oil on canvas, 1909. Ernst Ludwig Kirchner, German. W. 94. Contemporary Collection of The Cleveland Museum of Art and

Bequest of William R. Valentiner. 66.49

Fox. Etching, 1911. Georges Braque, French. H. 54.8. Gift of The Print Club of Cleveland. 59.225

Orpheus. Pastel, after 1913. Odilon Redon, French. H. 69.8. Gift from J. H. Wade. 26.25

Gypsy Child. Graphite and watercolor, 1916. Egon Schiele, Austrian. H. 49.9. Severance and Greta Millikin Collection. 64.285

Nude on the Shore. Woodcut on green paper, colored by hand, 1913, state I/II. Erich Heckel, German. H. 50.6. Andrew R. and Martha Holden Jennings Fund. 86.16

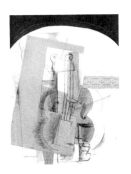

Still Life with Violin. Collage with gouache and charcoal on chipboard, ca. 1913. Georges Braque, French. H. 71.8. Leonard C. Hanna, Jr., Fund. 68.196

The Judgment of Paris. Bronze, dated 1914. Pierre Auguste Renoir (and Richard Guino), French. W. 89.4. Purchase from the J. H. Wade Fund. 41.591

Self-Portrait with Hat and Coat. Oil on canvas, dated 1915. Lovis Corinth, German. H. 99.7. Leonard C. Hanna, Jr., Fund. 79.14

Markwippach. Oil on canvas, dated 1917. Lyonel Feininger, American (b. Germany). W. 101. Gift of Julia, wife of Lyonel Feininger. 60.180

Male Torso. Brass, dated 1917. Constantin Brancusi, Romanian, French school. H. 46.7. Hinman B. Hurlbut Collection. 3205.37

Markwippach III. Charcoal, 1917. Lyonel Feininger, American (b. Germany). W. 25.5. Gift of Mrs. Lyonel Feininger. 63.73

Dancing Sailors. Watercolor, 1917. Charles Demuth, American. W. 25.4. Mr. and Mrs. William H. Marlatt Fund. 80.9

Church Bells Ringing, Rainy Winter Night. Watercolor, 1917. Charles Burchfield, American. H. 76.2. Gift of Mrs. Louise M. Dunn in memory of Henry G. Keller. 49.544

Figures. Pen and black ink, watercolor, and gouache, over graphite, 1921. Wyndham Lewis, British. H. 50.2. Leonard C. Hanna, Jr., Fund. 85.12

Harlequin with Violin (Si Tu Veux). Oil on canvas, 1918. Pablo Picasso, Spanish, French school. H. 142.2. Leonard C. Hanna, Jr., Fund. 75.2

Church Street El. Oil on canvas, 1920. Charles R. Sheeler, Jr., American. W. 48.5. Mr. and Mrs. William H. Marlatt Fund. 77.43

Interior: The Brown Tea Pot. Oil on canvas, ca. 1924. Gwen John, British. H. 33. Mr. and Mrs. William H. Marlatt Fund. 82.6

Forest. Painted wood, 1916. Jean (Hans) Arp, French (Alsatian). W. 58.8. Contemporary Collection of The Cleveland Museum of Art. 70.52

The Aviator (L'Aviateur). Oil on canvas, 1920. Fernand Léger, French. W. 92.5. Leonard C. Hanna, Jr., Fund. 81.16

Self-Portrait with Hat. Oil on canvas, 1919. Karl Schmidt-Rottluff, German. H. 73.3. Bequest of William R. Valentiner. 65.440

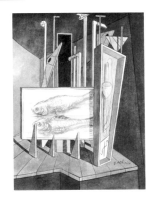

Water Lilies. Oil on canvas, ca. 1919-22. Claude Oscar Monet, French. W. 425.3. John L. Severance Fund. 60.81

Metaphysical Interior (Interieur Metaphysique). Oil on canvas, 1917. Giorgio de Chirico, Italian (b. Greece). H. 71.5. John L. Severance Fund. 81.51

Veranda Column with Two Figures. Painted wood, ca. 1920. Agbonbiofe Adeshina, Nigerian, Yoruba, Ekiti. H. 106.7. James Albert and Mary Gardiner Ford Memorial Fund. 69.55

The Dessert. Oil on canvas, 1921. Pierre Bonnard, French. H. 80. Gift of the Hanna Fund. 49.18

Versailles. Photograph, arrowroot printing-out paper, gold toned, 1922-23. Eugène Atget, French. W. 22.6. John L. Severance Fund. 85.113

Kestnermappe 6: Construction. Lithograph, 1923. László Moholy-Nagy, Hungarian. H. 59.4. Purchase from the J. H. Wade Fund. 89.16

Antelope Headdress. Wood with metal, shells, and beads. Africa, Mali, Bamana, Bamako area, ca. 1920s. H. 44.5. Gift of Mrs. Ralph M. Coe in memory of Ralph M. Coe. 65.325

Hook Figure. Painted wood and cowrie shell. Melanesia, Papua New Guinea, Central Sepik River District, Arambak People, ca. 1920-30. H. 207. Gift of Edgar A. Hahn. 63.553

Still Life. Oil on canvas. Preston Dickinson, American, 1891-1930. W. 76.5. Hinman B. Hurlbut Collection. 1664.26

Still Life with Biscuits. Oil and sand on canvas, dated 1924. Pablo Picasso, Spanish, French school. W. 100.7. Leonard C. Hanna, Jr., Fund. 78.45

Carnival at Nice. Oil on canvas, ca. 1923. Henri Matisse, French. W. 95.3. Mr. and Mrs. William H. Marlatt Fund. 46.444

Paris from My Window. Photograph, gelatin silver print, 1926. André Kertész, American (b. Hungary). H. 27.9. Gift of Max and Betty Ratner. 85.63

Terminal Tower, Cleveland. Photograph, gelatin silver print, 1928. Margaret Bourke-White, American. H. 34.1. Gift of Max and Betty Ratner. 85.76

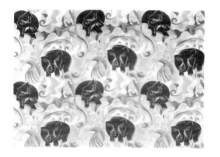

Elephants (detail). Patterned weave, Jacquard loom; silk and metal threads. France, 1924. Designed by Raoul Dufy. Overall L. 237. Gift of J. H. Wade. 26.557

Hills, South Truro. Oil on canvas, 1930. Edward Hopper, American. W. 109.5. Hinman B. Hurlbut Collection. 2647.31

Pensive Face. Cut-out iron mounted on painted wood, 1929. Julio Gonzalez, Spanish. H. 24.5. Gift of Ralph King by exchange. 80.32

Vase. Glass, ca. 1928. Maurice Marinot, French. H. 25.2. Gift of C. M. de Hauke. 29.114

Covered Jar. Porcelain, designed 1929, executed 1930-31. Agnes Moreau-Jouin (designer of decoration), French, Sèvres. H. 45.1. John L. Severance Fund. 87.196

Portrait of Josef May. Mixed
media on board,1926. Otto Dix,
German. H. 100. Purchase from
the J. H. Wade Fund. 85.40

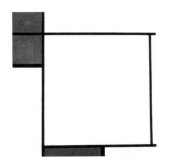

*Composition with Red, Yellow,
and Blue.* Oil on canvas, 1927.
Piet Mondrian, Dutch. H. 51.1.
Contemporary Collection of
The Cleveland Museum of Art.
67.215

Autumn Landscape. Lithograph,
1926. Emil Nolde, German.
W. 80.8. Fiftieth Anniversary
Gift of The Print Club of
Cleveland. 70.353

Male Figure. Wood. Africa,
Zaire, Sikasingo, Upper Lualaba
area, ca. 1920s. H. 48.2. Gift of
Katherine C. White. 69.10

*Mountain Landscape with Fir
Trees.* Graphite, brush and India
ink, ca. 1918-29. Ernst Ludwig
Kirchner, German. W. 50.6.
Delia E. Holden and L. E.
Holden Funds. 63.86

Mother and Child. Wood. Africa,
Ivory Coast, Senufo, Korhogo
area, ca. 1930. H. 63.5. James
Albert and Mary Gardiner Ford
Memorial Fund. 61.198

Grade Society Figure. Fern-
wood. Melanesia, Ambrym
Island, Vanuatu (New
Hebrides), ca. 1930. H. 210.9.
Gift of Herbert Baker. 71.272

*Rock and Sea, Small Point,
Maine.* Oil on canvas, 1931.
John Marin, American. W. 71.
Norman O. Stone and Ella A.
Stone Memorial Fund. 56.361

Circus Horses. Oil on canvas,
dated 1933. Clarence Holbrook
Carter, American. W. 91.4. Gift
of Lillian M. Kern. 80.302

Nocturne. Oil on copper, dated
1935. Joan Miró, Spanish. H. 42.
Mr. and Mrs. William H. Marlatt
Fund. 78.61

The Spinach Tree. Watercolor,
1934. William Sommer, American. W. 50.8. Gift of Dr. and Mrs.
Theodor W. Braasch. 61.324

Hand and Wheel. Photograph,
gelatin silver print, 1933. Alfred
Stieglitz, American. H. 24.1.
Gift of Cary Ross, Knoxville,
Tennessee. 35.99

Untitled. Photograph, gelatin
silver print, 1934. Edward
Weston, American. W. 28. John
L. Severance Fund. 84.168

*Bubble Emerging from Clay Pipe
and Frosted Leaf.* Photograph,
rayograph (gelatin silver print),
1937. Man Ray (Emmanuel
Rudnitsky), American. H. 39.9.
John L. Severance Fund. 84.23

*Constellation: Woman with
Blond Armpit Combing Her
Hair by the Light of the Stars.*
Gouache and oil, 1940. Joan
Miró, Spanish. W. 46. Contem-
porary Collection of The
Cleveland Museum of Art. 65.2

Pendant of a Male Elder. Cast gold. Africa, Ivory Coast, Baule, ca. 1930s. H. 7.5. John L. Severance Fund. 54.602

Mask. Wood and fiber. Africa, Zaire, Yaka, ca. 1930s. H. 47. Gift of Katherine C. White. 69.8

Guitar and Bottle of Marc on a Table. Oil and sand on canvas, 1930. Georges Braque, French. H. 129. Leonard C. Hanna, Jr., Fund. 75.59

Mask. Wood and pigment. Africa, Zaire, Songye, ca. 1930s. H. 71.2. Purchase from the J. H. Wade Fund. 72.2

Bull's Skull, Fruit, Pitcher. Oil on canvas, 1939. Pablo Picasso, Spanish, French school. W. 91.6. Leonard C. Hanna, Jr., Fund. 85.57

Snake Headdress. Painted wood. Africa, Guinea, Baga, ca. 1930s. H. 148. The Norweb Collection. 60.37

War Shield. Painted wood. Melanesia, Irian Jaya, New Guinea, Asmat People, ca. 1940. H. 176.5. Gift of The May Company. 63.554

Landscape. Oil and pencil on canvas, 1943. Arshile Gorky, American (b. Armenia). W. 63.5. Contemporary Collection of The Cleveland Museum of Art. 63.152

Dead Tree with Pink Hill. Oil on canvas, 1945. Georgia O'Keeffe, American. W. 102.2. Bequest of Georgia O'Keeffe. 87.138

Figure. Oil on cardboard, 1949. Willem de Kooning, American (b. Holland). H. 46.7. Contemporary Collection of The Cleveland Museum of Art. 64.1

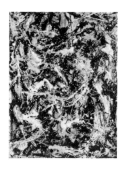

Number 5, 1950. Oil on canvas. Jackson Pollock, American. H. 136.5. Leonard C. Hanna, Jr., Fund. 80.180

Pilgrim. Steel, 1957. David Smith, American. H. 207. Contemporary Collection of The Cleveland Museum of Art. 66.385

Untitled. Painted metal, ca. 1958-59. John Chamberlain, American. H. 82.4. Andrew R. and Martha Holden Jennings Fund. 73.27

Untitled. Welded steel, 1961. Richard Stankiewicz, American. H. 170.2. Gift of The Cleveland Society for Contemporary Art in honor of Edward B. Henning and Purchase from the J. H. Wade Fund. 86.80

Gloria. Oil and paper collage on canvas, 1956. Robert Rauschenberg, American. H. 168.3. Gift of The Cleveland Society for Contemporary Art. 66.333

Sleeper I. Oil on canvas, 1958. Philip Guston, American (b. Canada). W. 193. Contemporary Collection of The Cleveland Museum of Art. 61.21

Crest. Oil on canvas, 1958. Jack Tworkov, American (b. Poland). H. 190.5. Contemporary Collection of The Cleveland Museum of Art. 62.33

Sky Cathedral-Moon Garden Wall. Wood, painted black, 1956-59. Louise Nevelson, American (b. Russia). H. 217.5. Gift of The Mildred Andrews Fund. 74.76

Smaragd, Red, and Germinating Yellow. Oil on canvas, 1959. Hans Hofmann, American (b. Germany). H. 139.7. Contemporary Collection of The Cleveland Museum of Art. 60.57

Reconstruction. Encaustic and canvas collage on canvas, dated 1959. Jasper Johns, American. H. 155. Purchase, Accessions Reserve Fund and Andrew R. and Martha Holden Jennings Fund. 73.28

The Family Luzzara. Photograph, gelatin silver print, 1953. Paul Strand, American. W. 15. Leonard C. Hanna, Jr., Fund. 85.95

Head. Oil on canvas, 1951. Francis Bacon, British. H. 62.9. Leonard C. Hanna, Jr., Fund. 82.56

Interior with Etruscan Vase. Oil on canvas, dated 1940. Henri Matisse, French. W. 130.2. Gift of the Hanna Fund. 52.153

Square Platter: Birds in Snow. Stoneware, molded and cut with underglaze and overglaze decoration. Kitaoji Rosanjin, Japanese, 1883-1959. W. 30.5. Gift of Marion Hammer in memory of N. V. Hammer. 82.165

Mask with Female Figure. Wood. Africa, Mali, Dogon, Sanga area, ca. 1940. H. 111.2. James Albert and Mary Gardiner Ford Memorial Fund. 60.169

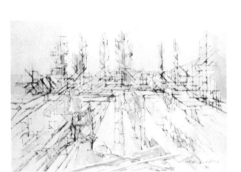

Video. Construction of mixed media. Joseph Cornell, American, 1903-72. W. 36.8. Contemporary Collection of The Cleveland Museum of Art. 64.143

Potager à la Brunié (Kitchen Garden at Brunie). Oil on canvas, dated 1941. Jacques Villon, French. W. 92. Leonard C. Hanna, Jr., Fund. 64.95

Mask. Painted wood. Africa, Burkina Faso, Nuna, ca. 1940s. H. 69.8. Gift of Katherine C. White. 69.2

Untitled (The Pincushion Man). Photograph, gelatin silver print, 1961. Diane Arbus, American. H. 29.7. Gift of Mr. and Mrs. Thomas A. Mann. 87.179

Untitled. Brush and black ink, 1959. Barnett Newman, American. W. 61. Purchase from the J. H. Wade Fund. 86.4

Number 99. Acrylic on canvas, 1959. Morris Louis, American. W. 360.6. Contemporary Collection of The Cleveland Museum of Art. 68.110

Elegy to the Spanish Republic. Oil on canvas, 1955-60. Robert Motherwell, American. W. 193.3. Contemporary Collection of The Cleveland Museum of Art. 63.583

Accent Grave. Oil on canvas, 1955. Franz Kline, American. H. 191.1. Anonymous Gift. 67.3

Composition Concrete (Study for Mural). Oil on canvas, 1957-60. Stuart Davis, American. H. 108.7. Contemporary Collection of The Cleveland Museum of Art. 64.2

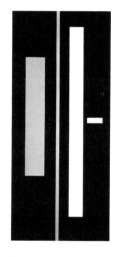

Ale Cans. Lithograph, 1964, proof. Jasper Johns, American. H. 35.6. Leonard C. Hanna, Jr., Fund. 85.55

Untitled. Black ink and enamel, 1965. Adolph Gottlieb, American. H. 61.1. Edwin R. and Harriet Pelton Perkins Memorial Fund. 87.48

Composites: Philadelphia (Apertures). Photograph, gelatin silver prints, 1965. Ray K. Metzker, American. W. 76.2. Purchase from the J. H. Wade Fund. 86.93

First Theme. Oil on canvas, 1963. Burgoyne Diller, American. H. 228.6. Andrew R. and Martha Holden Jennings Fund. 73.211

Fragmented Figure Construction. Welded steel, 1963. Richard Hunt, American. H. 143.5. Gift of Arnold H. Maremont. 69.16

Untitled. Acrylic on canvas, 1969. Larry Poons, American (b. Japan). H. 342.9. Gift of Agnes Gund. 69.49

Red Blue. Oil on canvas, 1962. Ellsworth Kelly, American. H. 228.6. Contemporary Collection of The Cleveland Museum of Art. 64.142

Louis II. Oil on canvas, 1962. Richard Lindner, American (b. Germany). H. 127. Contemporary Collection of The Cleveland Museum of Art. 65.450

Red Maroons. Oil on canvas, 1962. Mark Rothko, American (b. Russia). W. 205.7. Contemporary Collection and Friends of The Cleveland Museum of Art. 62.239

Three-Way Piece No. 2: Archer. Bronze, 1964. Henry Spencer Moore, British. H. 88.3. Anonymous Gift. 70.112

Still Life under a Lamp. Linoleum cut, 1962. Pablo Picasso, Spanish, French school. W. 64. John L. Severance Fund. 84.61

Impala. Oil on canvas, 1968. Alex Katz, American. W. 276.9. Mr. and Mrs. William H. Marlatt Fund and Gift of the Eppler Family Foundation and Agnes Gund. 83.68

Plate. Earthenware, 1968. Maria Martinez and Popovi Da, Native American, New Mexico, San Ildefonso Pueblo. D. 26.4. Gift of Various Donors by exchange. 70.508

Grey Pilgrim. Acrylic on canvas, 1971. Kenneth Noland, American. H. 240. Contemporary Collection of The Cleveland Museum of Art. 72.250

Jar. Earthenware, 1970. Fannie Nampeyo, Native American, Arizona, Hopi. H. 20.6. The Harold T. Clark Educational Extension Fund. 70.530

The Red Light. Plaster and mixed media, 1972. George Segal, American. H. 289.5. Andrew R. and Martha Holden Jennings Fund. 74.22

Moving Out. Photograph, gelatin silver prints and acrylic paint, 1962-84. Robert Frank, American (b. Switzerland). W. 369.6. John L. Severance Fund. 87.128

Wrapping It Up at the Lafayette. Collage, acrylic, and lacquer, 1974. Romare Bearden, American. H. 122. Mr. and Mrs. William H. Marlatt Fund. 85.41

Female Model on African Stool. Oil on canvas, 1976. Philip Pearlstein, American. H. 182.8. Mr. and Mrs. William H. Marlatt Fund. 78.16

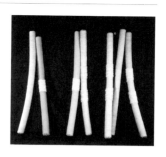

Available Forms. Weaving and wrapping; wool and synthetics, 1976. Jean Stamsta, American. H. 285. Gift of The Textile Arts Club. 77.187

Rock Carvings: Passage of the Seasons. Basalt with mineral accretions, 1981. Isamu Noguchi, American. H. 287. Gift of the Mildred Andrews Fund. 81.46

Sunset and Concrete Dock. Oil on canvas, painted wood, and concrete, 1984. Jennifer Bartlett, American. H. 330.5. John L. Severance Fund. 85.206

Mixteca Series No. 12. Collage and couching; Mexican *ixtle* (unspun), *amate*, acrylic, and cotton on linen, 1984. Evelyn Svec Ward, American. H. 26. Wishing Well Fund. 84.73

Untitled XIII. Oil on canvas, 1985. Willem de Kooning, American (b. Holland). H. 203.2. Leonard C. Hanna, Jr., Fund. 87.63

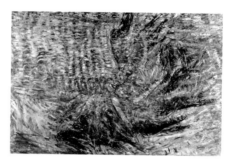

Vaulting. Oil on canvas, 1986-87. Susan Rothenberg, American. W. 336.5. Leonard C. Hanna, Jr., Fund. 88.12

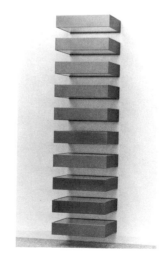

Untitled. Green anodized aluminum and clear plexiglass, 1989. Donald Judd, American. W. each of 10 units 68.6. Dorothea Wright Hamilton Fund. 90.18

Ocean Park No. 109. Oil on canvas, 1978. Richard Diebenkorn, American. H. 254. Marlatt Fund and gift of Society for Contemporary Art and an anonymous donor. 79.17

Portrait of IB. Oil on canvas, 1978. Lucian Freud, British (b. Germany). H. 50.7. Mr. and Mrs. William H. Marlatt Fund. 79.15

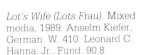

Myth of the Western Man. Ceramic, redwood, and painted wood, 1986. Robert Arneson, American. H. 221.6. Leonard C. Hanna, Jr., Fund. 87.55

Speakers. Photograph, gelatin silver print, hand-colored, 1983. Gilbert, British, and George, British. W. 403.9. John L. Severance Fund. 84.170

Lot's Wife (Lots Frau). Mixed media, 1989. Anselm Kiefer, German. W. 410. Leonard C. Hanna, Jr., Fund. 90.8

Vessel. Stoneware with ash glaze. Tsujimura Shujiro, b. 1948, Japanese. D. 35.7. Gift of Dr. and Mrs. Daniel Verne in honor of Dr. and Mrs. Sherman E. Lee; the Gallery Group and various donors in honor of Sherman E. Lee; in honor of Dr. and Mrs. Sherman E. Lee's 50th Anniversary (monies previously given); and John L. Severance Fund. 90.19

Untitled. Bronze, 1989. Joel Shapiro, American. W. 203.2. Leonard C. Hanna, Jr., Fund. 89.57

Only individual artists are included in this index, since the Handbook is organized by period and geographic area.

For CMA 32.537, *Quadrilobed Plaque* by Circle of Guillaume Julien, the full credit line is: The Mary Spedding Milliken Memorial Collection, gift of William Mathewson Milliken.

For CMA 40.465, *Study for the Nude Youth* by Michelangelo Buonarroti, the full credit line is: Gift in memory of Henry G. Dalton by his nephews George S. Kendrick and Harry D. Kendrick.

For CMA 57.496, *Pope Innocent X* by Allessandro Algardi, the full credit line is: Gift of Rosenberg & Stiebel, Inc., in honor of William Mathewson Milliken, Director, 1930-58.

For CMA 64.170, *Arrow Vase with Persian Inscriptions*, China, Ming dynasty, the full credit line is: Severance and Greta Millikin Collection.